THE FIRST MISTAKE

THE FIRST MISTAKE

AMERICA IN VIETNAM, 1945-1954

J. Edward Lee, Ph.D.

Charleston, SC
www.PalmettoPublishing.com

The First Mistake

Hardcover ISBN: 978-1-64990-316-7
Paperback ISBN: 978-1-64990-315-0
eBook ISBN: 978-1-64990-314-3

For my grandchildren: Madeline Ann and Connor Robert Walen.

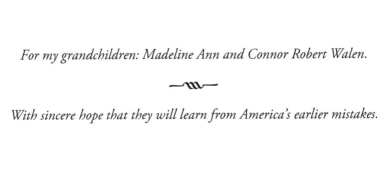

With sincere hope that they will learn from America's earlier mistakes.

ACKNOWLEDGEMENTS

P ROJECTS SUCH AS *The First Mistake* are impossible without the assistance and encouragement of key people. The relationship between the United States and Vietnam seems to be on the road of reconciliation. I sensed the early stages of this positive development while researching my two earlier books. Perhaps we share a common enemy in today's world. Teacher Vy My of Ben Tre represents the birth of this friendship. She supplied me with visual images of her beautiful homeland, which included French architecture. Poet Dang Than of Hanoi confirmed that agents from the Office of Strategic Services and Ho Chi Minh had formed a close relationship in 1945, a missed opportunity. Professor Ha Nguyen of Duy Tan University in Da Nang confirmed the potency of dnationalism and independence which flows through his country.

In America, my friend, Joseph Galloway, is a towering figure in journalism. His heroic experiences in 1965 at Ia Drang Valley with a greatly outnumbered American force resulted in the book *We Were Soldiers* which he wrote with Hal Moore and became a Hollywood blockbuster starring Mel Gibson. Joseph continues to be a champion for the warriors of the Vietnam conflict, reminding us of their sacrifices. He, also, confirmed that Ho and the Americans could have taken a different path in 1945 with the encouragement of apparently disinterested Washington policymakers. I appreciate his assistance early in this research.

My retired Winthrop University colleague, Dr. Jason Silverman, an Abraham Lincoln scholar, has been my friend for three decades. He and I share similar views on many things, and I appreciate his suggestions as this endeavor neared conclusion. We both were elected officials at one time, and we both understand that academics must reach beyond the Ivory Towers.

My parents, Tyre Douglas Lee, Sr. and Ola Bankhead Lee introduced me to history at an early age. They were Giants, members of what NBC News' Tom Brokaw superbly labeled "the greatest generation." My father, who was Old Army, graduating from Infantry School at Fort Benning, Georgia in 1931, found himself swimming ashore at Normandy in the summer of 1944. Returning to South Carolina, he heeded my teacher mother's advice and became a police officer, leading a small southern town through the tumultuous 1960s. He and my mother took my brother, Tyre D. Lee, Jr., a Vietnam War veteran, and me to the state of Virginia when we were youngsters, visiting the home places of our Lee ancestors at Arlington and Stratford Hall, homes that had been lost when earlier generations made their own mistakes.

Dr. Hugh Charles "Toby" Haynsworth, a retired naval commander who became a College of Business professor at Winthrop University, helped immensely with my first two Vietnam books, opening doors and sharing contacts which were invaluable. He, and his wife, Martha Bragg Haynsworth became friends who laid the groundwork for *The First Mistake*.

Mentors inspire us, and I have benefitted from the wisdom of quite a few: Drs. Thomas S. Morgan, Ross A, Webb, James C. Casada, Birdsall S. Viault, John J. Duffy, Lacy K. Ford, Robert Weir, Edward Cox, and George C. Rogers, Jr. All through graduate school and beyond, these people offered advice which helped prepare me for my own thirty-six-year career. Mentors at Winthrop University include some of the above and Professor Ron J. Chepesiuk, a prolific writer and archivist. David Goldfield of the University of North Carolina-Charlotte continues as a mentor, as he explores the twentieth century.

Early in my career, I brushed up against some of the towering figures in my profession: Arthur M. Schlesinger who was at Hofstra University when I presented a paper at the 50th anniversary of Pearl Harbor Conference, Stephen Ambrose who chatted with me in 1990 at the University of Kansas when I presented at the Dwight Eisenhower Conference, and George Brown Tindal who advised me, "Always teach the United States Survey courses." I have followed that advice.

Just as I have benefitted from the wisdom of mentors, I have shared advice with exceptional graduate students. Some have gone on to write their own books: Deann Segal, Gwen Shealy, Sandi Ludwa, Tally Johnson, and Buddy Motz. Others are not far behind: Marlana Mayton and her research about Winthrop students who helped break the Nazi code in World War II and Ozlem Karakas of Turkey and her fresh look at the 1915 Armenian genocide.

Finally, as always and most importantly, I thank my wife, Ann-Franklin Hardy Lee, and daughter, Elizabeth Ann Lee Walen, who have always been supportive of my love of history. They both know that I love them best of all.

TABLE OF CONTENTS

INTRODUCTION

"It is well that war is so terrible or we should grow too fond of it."

—Robert E. Lee, 1862

O NE OF MY graduate history courses at Winthrop University is called "America At War." We commence with the American Revolution and conclude with our response to 9/11. I stress to the students that the Framers of the United States Constitution set forth a clear mechanism for sending our sons and daughters into combat. The president requests a Declaration of War, making the case, and the Congress debates and approves (or rejects) it by a 2/3 vote. We have followed that clear procedure exactly five times: 1812, 1846, 1898, 1917, and 1941. Usually, we ignore our Constitution, as Abraham Lincoln did with his undeclared war in 1861 and in Korea and Vietnam. More often, 300 times, we have expended blood and treasure without a formal Declaration of War.

Each year as I teach that course, I am cognizant of the fact that most of my students have never lived in a period of peace. From the aftermath of the terrorist attacks of September 11, 2001, our nation has been at war, specifically in Afghanistan and Iraq. While our educational institution offers a minor in Peace Studies, the reality is that war in faraway places has shaped the lives of today's college students. As I reflect on my nearly four decades in the university classroom, wars and rumors of wars have hovered over my career and the material I teach. My research seems to perpetually become ensnarled in battles and the sacrifices of men and women who find themselves facing the enemy, often an enemy like the Taliban in Afghanistan or the Viet Cong, who faded into the countryside of Vietnam. Death and destruction haunt my curriculum.

My earlier books have demonstrated the pervasive presence of war in my academic career. *South Carolina In The Civil War: The Confederate Experience* (McFarland, 2003) attempted to explain the impact that conflict had on my native state and the carnage and debris left behind by four devastating years. I sought an answer to the key questions, "Why did the Confederates fight?" "What were their objectives?" "Why did they risk everything?" "Did they not see that slavery was immoral?" "Did they believe the Constitution gave them the right to secede?" Two chapters in that book examined the effect on my great-great grandfather, Confederate Captain Obadiah Hardin, the grandson of a sixteen-year-old hero from the 1780 Battle of Kings Mountain. In his war, Captain Hardin fell in December 1861 at the Battle of Dranesville, Virginia, clenching the southern flag in his hands. My book includes his correspondence with his wife, Paulina Worthy Hardin, the daughter of a wealthy slave-owner, who, after Captain Hardin fell, was left to raise five young children. It was a costly war, fought over the unfair system of human bondage and intertwined in the South's belief in its right to secede. That war wrecked many lives, including Widow Hardin and the fatherless Hardin children.

In 2011, I published *Southern Cold Warrior: Congressman James P. Richards* Richards (Xlibris, 2011). This work was a study of an influential South Carolinian who fought in France in 1918, came home and earned a law degree and entered politics, first as probate judge of Lancaster County and, in 1932, as a New Deal Democratic Congressman. Richards split with President Franklin D. Roosevelt, however, in November 1941 as the latter requested revisions in the Neutrality Act which would have allowed more aid to reach the beleaguered United Kingdom. Standing on the floor of the

House of Representatives, Richards lambasted the president's "through-the-back-door-war." Richards had witnessed close up in 1918 the horrors of war as a member of the Old Hickory Division in France, and he saw America, in the autumn of 1941, ill-prepared for another international conflict. Emotionally, he told his colleagues, "America comes first with me!"

After the attack at Pearl Harbor a few weeks later, Congressman Richards tried to re-enlist in the United States army, but FDR requested that he remain in Washington. By 1945, Richards had become a senior member of the house Foreign Affairs Committee. He, like Presidents Harry Truman and Dwight Eisenhower, became a Cold Warrior, sensing the evil coming from the Soviet Union. Serving four years in the 1950s as chair of his committee, Richards ended his career in 1957 as a special ambassador, travelling 30,000 miles on behalf of Eisenhower and Secretary of State john Foster Dulles, explaining the threats posed by "international communism," dispensing millions of dollars in American aid to fifteen Middle East countries as spokesperson for the Eisenhower Doctrine, an initiative to keep oil under the control of the West. Interestingly, Richards saw the Cold War as a conflict between the United States and Soviet Union which ignored Southeast Asia. To Richards, France's desire in the post-World War II era to cling to its Asian colonies should not be of concern to us. Europe and the Middle East were far more strategic, the congressman believed, than propping up an unjust Asian colony which benefited only France at the expense of the Vietnamese people.

My two Vietnam War books, *White Christmas In April: The Collapse Of South Vietnam,* 1975 (Peter Lang Publishing, 1999) and *Nixon, Ford And The Abandonment Of South Vietnam* (McFarland Publishing, 2002) hold politicians accountable for poor and costly decisions which wrecked lives and inflicted pain on Americans and Vietnamese. Furthermore, our international reputation was severely damaged. These two studies generated my interest in how wars end, in the specific case of Vietnam, 1973-1975. Lessons of honor, courage, duplicity, and shortsightedness litter the battlefields of

Southeast Asia. Those two books, drawing on more than 100 interviews with Asian and American sources, document the foreign policy mess which Vietnam had become for the United States in the war's last years.

So, my students and I share our thoughts about American wars and how decisions, perhaps well-intended, can go astray and create wounds which are slow to heal. Thus, General Robert E. Lee's 1862 observation at the Battle of Fredericksburg as the Confederates decimated charging Union troops commanded by General Ambrose Burnside is worth pondering yet again, until we perhaps better understand it. Why do we stumble into wars, mostly undeclared? Must we send our valiant troops everywhere? What, exactly, are our country's interests? Who shapes foreign policy? How do we identify friends and enemies? What should we learn from America's own history of war? Should we not heed the American public? Those are just a few of the important questions sparked by a review of the American journey since 1776.

Almost 2500 years ago, the Athenian historian and general Thucydides wrote of his state's war, the clash between Athens and Sparta which we know as the Peloponnesian War (431-404 B.C.) .He suggested that wars are triggered by honor, fear, and interest. Perhaps the ancient historian, like the more recent Confederate general at Fredericksburg, understood essential truths. What, exactly, are a country's interests? When do fear and honor become irrational? While history does not repeat itself, it does whisper to us, and we should listen closely to its voice. With that in mind, let us consider the Vietnam War one more time, how the conflict began instead of how it ended. That is the purpose of *The First Mistake: America In Vietnam, 1945-1954* . The initial error was misunderstanding the obvious: our nation's own historical tradition, nurtured in a fight for independence, should have provided us guidance for avoiding the catastrophe which cost America 58,318 men and women, fracturing the body politick, demolishing our invincibility, and haunting us for decades. We commence our analysis with a visit to the wall in our capital city where the names of the 58,318 speak to us.

NOT YOUR MISTAKES

"The only things one never regrets are one's mistakes."
—Oscar Wilde, 1891

M Y LATE WINTHROP University colleague, Dr. Hugh C. "Toby" Haynsworth, III, and I became friends in 1994. His career as a professor of quantitative methods and computer science began after two decades as a naval officer. Graduating from the University of North Carolina with a degree in music, Toby Haynsworth was the son of a rear admiral who had served in World War II and the Korean police action. Rising through the ranks in the United States Navy, Toby Haynsworth found himself assigned as the supply officer on the *USS Midway* off the coast of South Vietnam in April 1975, as the communists advanced on Saigon. Commander Toby Haynsworth witnessed the evacuation of that country, helicopters full of refugees and their families landing on the *Midway's* deck and small vessels crammed with others heading toward the American ships off the coast of South Vietnam. Throughout the last days of April 1975, they continued to flee. One woman who Toby and I interviewed arrived with a quarter in her pocket. Another man, piloting a small plane, made an emergency landing on the deck of the *Midway,* surviving along with his family.

Commander Haynsworth's experiences in 1975 helped generate interest in a second career in academia. Retiring from the navy, he earned a doctorate from Clemson University. So, twenty years after Operation Frequent Wind, the heroic evacuation of more than 150,000 South Vietnamese and the exodus of the remaining Americans, in the spring of 1975, Dr. Haynsworth and I began a friendship and partnership which produced two books: *White Christmas In April: The Collapse Of South Vietnam, 1975* and *Nixon, Ford And The Abandonment Of South Vietnam* .We interviewed more than 100 men and women, Americans and Vietnamese, recorded their experiences, and used primary documents to tell their stories of the period 1973-1975.

The first book chronicled the courage and chaos of America's longest war. Our research took us many places, and we interviewed a wide range of people: diplomats, Central Intelligence Agency operatives, enlisted men, generals, civilians, and the communist victors. Women as well as men were contacted, a woman who as an infant survived the early April 1975 tragic crash of Operation Baby Lift and the female payroll officer, Ann Hazard, who was tasked with making severance payments to loyal South Vietnamese, for example. The 1999 publication of *White Christman In April* generated tremendous interest as the twenty-fifth anniversary of Operation Frequent Wind approached in 2000.

Among the people we had interviewed were the last two commanders of American forces in South Vietnam: Generals John Murray and Homer Smith. Murray, an attorney, sitting in his Virginia home with his daughter at his side, leapt from his chair and shouted, "We could have won in Vietnam!" General Smith, who evacuated the country in the last hours of April 30, 1975, was more sedate. Living in San Antonio, Texas, the site of the Alamo, he supplied Toby Haynsworth and myself with tremendous insight into the deteriorating conditions in South Vietnam that spring. Another interviewee, Director of Housing Sally Vineyard, had succinctly explained it this way, "We were vacuuming up a country." One of our interviews was with General Alexander Haig, NATO commander in 1975, who flew to Washington from Brussels, Belgium in early April to meet with President Gerald Ford in the Oval Office. Haig pled for more military assistance, B-52s, which could terrify the communists. The commander-in-chief's response: "Al, the American people don't have the stomach for anymore of Vietnam." Haig rose and said, "Then you will be a one term president."

Murray, Hazard, Smith, Vineyard, and 100 other people had formed after the war the Saigon Mission Association (SMA), comprised of the last individuals to leave Southeast Asia and a few of their allies. Toby and I joined that organization as honorary members, and the contacts which we made were invaluable for our research. On April 30, 2000, I was invited by General Smith and the SMA to be part of a ceremony at the Vietnam War Memorial in Washington as the sun rose. As a historian, I was asked to make a few comments that April morning during the ceremony at the wall.

Dedicated in 1982 during the presidency of Ronald Reagan, the Vietnam Veterans Memorial, like the war itself, was not without controversy. Architect Maya Lin's design, two enormous black Indian granite walls with 144 panels on a two-acre site administered by the National Park Service, was criticized because of its stark simplicity. The walls, varying from a height of slightly over ten feet to a descent to only eight inches, stand on the National Mall, northeast of the Lincoln Memorial. In the distance is the Korean War Veterans Memorial, consisting of nineteen stainless steel oversize servicemen making their way across a field where 2500 images from that undeclared conflict await them. It may commemorate America's forgotten war, a United Nations authorized police action, but that overwhelming memorial seems almost alive.

Maya Linn's Vietnam Memorial is much more solemn; its power rests in its simplicity. The wall has attracted an estimated 5,000,000 visitors since President Reagan dedicated it. Pointing toward the Lincoln Memorial and the Washington Monument, the Vietnam Veterans Memorial regularly attracts survivors of that conflict, the families and friends of the 58,318 names etched on the panels, as well as curious tourists. It seems to be magnetized, a destination point in our capital city. Visitors leave mementos in honor of those who died: medals, photographs, letters, flowers. Diamonds are etched in recognition of the dead, and crosses designate status unknown. The names are chronological from 1956 to those killed in May 1975 during the *Mayaguez rescue* incident in Cambodia. Interestingly, Lieutenant Colonel A. Peter Dewey, an Office of Strategic Services operative who died in 1945 is not listed. We will discuss his role in our longest war later.

That April 2000 morning, I was reminded of the premise that Toby and I had as we began our research. We believed that a study of the conclusion of the war and an analysis of Operation of Frequent Wind could help us understand the conflict in its entirety. The heroism, improvising, confusion, politics, desperation, selfishness, flawed strategy, egos, bureaucracy, and gallantry of 1975 characterized the war from its beginning to end. I still believe that to be correct, but by focusing on the period from 1945-1954 we gain additional insight on how Vietnam became a morass, a defeat for the globe's greatest power. Why did we feel compelled to support French colonialism? What were our interests? Did we consider the potential costs?

The crowd the spring morning of April 30, 2000 was large. I sat next to General Smith, and he told me that a group of women associated with the ill-fated Operation Baby Lift of early April 1975, when a latch securing a C-5A transport carrying American nurses and Vietnamese babies had sprung open after liftoff from Saigon, spewing its human cargo as the plane made an emergency landing, had earlier commemorated that tragic event. Now, on April 30, 2000, I would make remarks at this ceremony at the wall.

As Homer Smith and I chatted, he leaned over to me and remarked, "I want to thank you for telling our story." My response: "" Thank you and the others for what you did for us in Vietnam." The notice and media coverage which accompanied the publication the previous year of *White Christmas In April* had been enabled by the sacrifices of the more than 58,000 names listed on Maya Lin's memorial and the millions more who served in uniforms from all branches as civilian employees during the war. During the ceremony, I briefly thanked those who assembled that spring day, the survivors and those who had paid the ultimate price. I spoke of their courage and patriotism. I ended my remarks by saying to those men and women who were now weeping or standing on crutches or missing limbs or wearing their old uniforms, "Mistakes were made. But you did not make them." The crowd applauded, and I vowed that I would continue researching and writing about their war, focusing on mistakes that had been made long before 1975.

THE SPIRIT OF '76

I N MY NEARLY four-decade long career, I have witnessed a rapidly changing world. In my cluttered office, I display a piece of the Berlin Wall, brought to me in 1989 by a student who served in the air national guard. Two years later, a lone Chinese student confronted a column of tanks in Tiananmen Square in Beijing. That photograph is in my collection, courage under fire. I sat in a Moscow McDonald's Restaurant in 1993 as a coup threatened the government of Russia's Boris Yeltsin. A photograph of me at that moment graces my bookshelf. I have vivid memories of teaching on the morning of September 11, 2001, a Tuesday, as planes slammed into the World Trade Center, the Pentagon, and a field in Pennsylvania. And, a fruitless search began for elusive Weapons of Mass Destruction and terrorists throughout the Middle East. These are prominent milestones in the twentieth century, and the United States has often been boldly on the right side of history (liberating Kuwait in 1991, for example). But sometimes we have demonstrated our ignorance of history. America's longest war heads the list. Policymakers can be brilliant, and they can disappoint us with their recklessness.

When it comes to understanding why, in April 2000, we gathered at the Vietnam Veterans Memorial, we would be well-advised to learn from America's own experience as a colony of Great Britain. We hungered for independence and self-determination. Those are human rights, valued around the globe, regardless of race or ethnicity. They were certainly on the minds of Vietnamese in 1945 as they fought Japanese invaders, worked closely with American operatives, and resisted a return to French colonialism. There is much to consider in our own country's revolutionary experience. Lessons which need advocates in positions of power at key moments, grasping the importance of simple values like those on display during the American Revolution. To ignore these lessons, we miss opportunities and we run the risk of finding ourselves paying steep unexpected prices which are assessed in "blood and treasure." So, let us ponder the experiences of our own Founding Fathers and what they might mean regarding the Vietnam War.

Two of the best-known American patriots from the nation's creation, Virginia's Thomas Jefferson and Massachusetts' John Adams spent decades first as collaborators, then as bitter rivals, and finally as statesmen. Their regions were in conflict, two very different societies and economies. The slaveocracy of the South which had 400,000 slaves in 1770 and the commercial and livestock farms of New England were in conflict because of the emphasis on large scale agriculture in the South, with its reliance on human bondage, and New England's merchants, small farms, and Boston harbor. As political parties evolved, the two Founding Fathers came, despite President George Washington's 1796 warning, to be leaders of competing factions: Adams a Federalist and Jefferson a Democratic-Republican. In foreign affairs, Adams favored Great Britain while Jefferson favored all things French as those two European powers fought each other for dominance in a never-ending war. Ultimately, the two men would compete for the presidency after Washington, exhausted, retired to Mount Vernon. When that 1796 election occurred, the young nation was split in partisanship with Adams triumphing and Jefferson settling for the vice-presidency under the Constitution as the document originally mandated. In the 1800 re-match, Jefferson was victorious narrowly, and Adams, placing third, left the new capital city before

Jefferson and Vice President Aaron Burr of New York were inaugurated. In his March 1801 speech, Jefferson commented, "We are all Americans," but the Federalists had left town in anger after filling the bureaucracy with Adams' supporters. Ultimately, Adams and Jefferson reconciled, corresponded, and, ironically, died on the same day, July 4, 1825. As the dying Adams sighed, "Jefferson still lives."

The two Americans had a long association and had witnessed the slide toward the American Revolution as Great Britain became more and more estranged from its colonies. In 1770, Adams, one of the best attorneys in the colonies, had represented the eleven British soldiers who, when discipline evaporated in snowy Boston in March, fired upon five protesters and became immortalized in silversmith Paul Revere's sketch of the Boston Massacre, a drawing which was used effectively by supporters of American independence. Both Adams and Jefferson would be appointed six years later by the Continental Congress to draft the Declaration of Independence. Adams, who admitted to being "obnoxious," deferred to the gifted wordsmith Jefferson, because, "You can write ten times better than the rest of us." It would be Mr. Jefferson's inspiring document which would so enthrall Vietnam's Ho Chi Minh in the 1930s and 1940s. I suggest that Ho believed in the essence of those lofty words: "All men are created equal…they are endowed by their Creator with certain unalienable rights, that among these are life, liberty, and the pursuit of happiness."

By 1776, Adams and Jefferson had witnessed the unfairness of a colonial system which benefitted Great Britain, much like the Indo Chinese system benefitted France. The colonies were treated as children by the Mother Country, supplying valuable natural resources and being denied actual representation in Parliament. The Church of England (Anglican) dominated the religious sphere in the British colonies similar to Roman Catholicism controlling Vietnam's Buddhists. Local officials were appointed by the legislatures back home in both cases. Mandarins owed their livelihood to France just as governmental bureaucrats in New York, Boston, Philadelphia, and Charleston served friends in Parliament. Clearly, this deeply entrenched second class system angered Jefferson and Adams here and, later, Ho and Vo Nguyen Giap in Vietnam.

Despite gross unfairness, however, revolutions do not just erupt, and wars of independence do not just occur. They build toward climax. That was true in the time of Jefferson and Adams and in the time of Ho and Giap. When General George Washington, with the help of the French fleet, trapped the Mother Country's Lord Charles Cornwallis at Yorktown in 1781, political and military efforts had been underway here in America for years. Similarly, when Ho Chi Minh and General Vo Nguyen Giap surrounded the French at Dien Bien Phu in 1954, shelling the French in the valley from the hills with artillery provided by China, that key battle was the culmination of decades of work by the Viet Minh forces.

Our own revolution evolved, also. With Great Britain controlling the vast natural wealth of timber, crops, and animal skins produced in America, Parliament protected its interests from the 1650s with a series of Navigation Acts which required the use of vessels from the Mother Country and a list of enumerated goods which benefitted England's economy. This one-sided relationship was far from fair, and by 1763 it became more onerous to the colonists. Victory over France in the Seven Year's War produced a stifling debt, estimated at 123,000,000 pounds with an additional 5,000,000 pounds in annual interest, wrecking Great Britain's economy. Parliament, which offered the Americans only virtual representation in policymaking saw the colonies as economic salvation. Legislation controlling movement into the fertile Ohio River Valley, which was gained by victory in the Seven Years' War, was passed-and ignored by colonists who reasoned that they were being treated as ungrateful children by King George III. That unpopular Proclamation Act, which stationed a standing army in the colonies to monitor things, was followed in 1764 by the Sugar Act and the Currency Act. These laws raised revenue for the indebted Mother Country, and, again, there was no actual Parliamentary representation. Smuggling was monitored and violators punished. Debts owed back home in England must be made in an approved currency. Similarly, France used the bountiful natural wealth of Vietnam as a source of revenue, administering through its Mandarin agents an economy which took rubber and coal from the Asians, as earlier French took spices. Soldiers bolstered the Mandarins, enforcing this unfair economic system.

In America, the 1765 Stamp Act placed a tax on legal documents, newspapers, pamphlets, contracts, licenses, ships' bills of sale, calendars, almanacs, and playing cards. King George's Stamp Act tax collectors, much like Vietnam's pro-French mandarins, were tarred and feathered by the Sons of Liberty who terrorized the tax collectors for serving the Mother Country. Harassment and beatings of these officials, who received 8% of Stamp Act revenue, occurred. In Vietnam, Ho's Viet Minh would be violent with those who collaborated with France, often beheading them.

A year later, Great Britain, lobbied by Benjamin Franklin who was popular on both sides of the Atlantic, repealed the despised Stamp Act, replacing it with the Declaratory Act, which clearly stated the intent of the Mother Country to be obeyed in the future. British troops would be quartered in colonists' home, open-ended search warrants issued, and violators tried in British-not colonial-courts. In Indochina, France would frequently dangle "self-government" in front of the Vietnamese teasing them with dreams of independence but never allowing them to leave France's orbit. Real power was consistently held by Paris, as Michelin built its rubber plantations across the land, sometimes land which were ancestral homelands to the Buddhists. As President Franklin D. Roosevelt explained in 1944, the French colony was "milked."

Throughout the lead up to the American Revolution, we, too, understood that England's colonies were being "milked." Great Britain's staggering debt from the Seven Years' War required more revenue-raising acts by Parliament.

The 1767 Townshend Acts placed taxes on lead, paper, glass, paint, as well as on tea. The Daughters of Liberty rose in resistance, every bit as brutal as the earlier Sons of Liberty. In Vietnam, women served as couriers, spies, and combatants, working in tandem with the men of Ho's Viet Minh. The Townshend Acts were repealed after the 1770 Boston Massacre-except for the duty on tea. A new piece of legislation called the Tea Act was passed by Parliament in 1773, igniting the Boston Tea Party that December, led by John Hancock and John Adams' cousin, Samuel Adams. The friends of King George III and Parliament, the East India Tea Company, found 342 chests of their product unceremoniously dumped in Boston Harbor by Hancock, Adams, and 150 of their accomplices. Parliament responded with the 1774 Coercive /Intolerable Acts, closing Boston Harbor, the site of many jobs, restricting the colony's local legislature, and demand that John Hancock and Samuel Adams be turned over to the Mother Country's judicial authorities. The other colonies rallied around Massachusetts as the Continental Congress convened in Philadelphia. The delegates compiled a list of grievances, much as Ho would do in Vietnam. A militia, the Minute Men, was formed. The following year, George Washington was named commander of a ragtag army. A clash occurred in April 1775 at Lexington and Concord.

By 1776, the Americans had suffered enough abuse, "milking" by the British. Independence was declared that summer, and the Revolution continued on battlefields from Saratoga (1777) to Valley Forge (1777-1778) to Kings Mountain (1780) to Cowpens (1781) to Yorktown (1781). Our revolution swelled, much like the one in Vietnam led by Ho, Giap, and their Viet Minh cadres, using guerrilla tactics and the assistance of other nations. In our case, France was seeking revenge for its defeat in the Seven Years' War. In Vietnam, Mao Zedong and the Soviet Union backed Ho. After 1949, Mao controlled China, and he wished a disciple in Vietnam. And, Ho, in the early 1930s, had studied Marxism in the Soviet Union.

I assert that a close examination of the earlier years of Ho's struggle to expel the French can be better understood if we remember our own lengthy struggle from Great Britain which matured into the Spirit of '76. We should recognize that self-determination and independence are powerful forces that motivate people differently across the globe. In the case of Indochina and Ho Chi Minh, we should be cognizant that the communists (of which Ho was one) were not monolithic. Initially, I argue that until 1945 and the return of French colonialism to Vietnam with our support, Ho was a nationalist, too. But our mistake that year in not building on a relationship which agents of the Office of Strategic Services had formed with Ho and Giap during World War II was a blunder. Ho, receiving Chinese and Soviet aid, abandoned nationalism and replaced it with full blown communism. As the late journalist Stanley Karnow wrote, Ho "saw the United States and its South Vietnamese allies as the continuation of two thousand years of resistance to Chinese and later French rule." Our first mistake occurred against the backdrop of the Second World War, which stained the reputation of France and gave us, in 1945, an opportunity which we did not take. To Ho, we would become just another colonial power, intent on "milking" Vietnam.

No Little Wars

"A great country can have no such thing as a little war."
—The Duke of Wellington, 1815

F RANCE WAS NOT the first foreign power to insert itself into Indochina. Before the Christian era, India and China eyed the lucrative spice trade and fertile terrain. By 900 A.D., China had won this competition, introducing rice cultivation to the populace. Trying to control their own destiny, the Vietnamese wrestled with the Mongols in the 1200s and defeated them in 1287 in the Red Valley, an area where Viet Minh commander General Vo Nguyen Giap, Ho's lieutenant, waged war against France in the early 1950s. The Chinese intruders stayed in towns, much like the French, while Vietnamese ruled the countryside. In 1426, the Vietnamese defeated China in a clash west of Hanoi. The country was divided into three regions: Tonkin in the north, Annam in the center, and Cochinchina around Saigon. From the 1500s until the 1700s, Vietnamese fought among themselves along a line similar to the boundary of north and south which divided the country in 1954 after the Geneva Conference.

As a Roman Catholic nation, France was motivated by missionary zeal and economic domination of the spice trade of pepper and nutmeg. It sent priests, entrepreneurs, and soldiers into Vietnam, seeking converts and business opportunities from the various factions. Left out of this increasing presence of foreign influence in Vietnam was the native population itself. In

1883, France, capitalizing on divisions among the three regions of Vietnam and among Buddhists and Catholics, formed a French "protectorate." The rural population resisted because they were employed at a pittance in unsafe coal mining. Opium was harvested in northern poppy fields, rice planted in the south, taxes levied without representation by the citizens, people uprooted from ancestral plots of land, and by the dawn of the twentieth century large rubber plantations were owned by French companies which supplied auto manufacturers. The "milking" of the Vietnamese economy was overseen by a Mandarin class of administrators, often French-educated and Roman Catholic. Thus, there was a collision of east and west in the "protectorate" of Vietnam, the French insensitive to Buddhism and the natives' preferences for small agricultural enterprises-as well as for independence. The Vietnamese adapted to the French presence in their country, but they resisted it, too.

Born in 1890 in Central Vietnam (Annam), the man who, after several name changes, would become known as Ho Chi Minh (Nguyen Tat Thanh) was enamored with western ideals of self-determination and independence. He was well-read, devouring western philosophy. After teaching for a few years, Ho in 1911 sailed on a French ship, visiting the American cities of San Francisco, Boston, and Brooklyn. His tour of the western world introduced the twenty-one year old to a vibrant democracy and a nation bustling with industry. He worked odd jobs, including as a baker, always keeping his eyes open to learn from a society which had once been a colony. His tour of the western world took him to London and Paris, where he attempted unsuccessfully to plead his case for Vietnam's independence to President Woodrow Wilson at the 1919 Paris Peace Conference, the site of discussions among the victors in the Great War of 1914-1918. At a meeting of French socialists in Tours, France the following year, Ho pleaded, "comrades, save us!" While Woodrow Wilson's commitment to self-determination of people's, espoused so eloquently in the president's 1918 Fourteen Points, apparently excluded the French colony of Vietnam, Ho hoped socialists in the French government would be more sympathetic. We should ponder race discrimination as a factor in both instances; Wilson was not progressive in all things, and the French government's socialists were not interested in this slender young Asian's dreams of independence for his homeland.

Ho's transformation from socialism to communism is significant. He recalled it this way: "it was patriotism and not communism that originally inspired me." Follow by French police, Ho realized that the socialists were not going to answer his calls for Vietnam's independence any more so than Woodrow Wilson, who had grown up in the American South with its racial barriers. Centuries of domination by China and France and the prosperity he had witnessed in the cities of the United States and Great Britain gave birth to a strain of Vietnamese communism by the early 1920s. In 1924, Ho moved to Moscow, meeting with Joseph Stalin and Leon Trotsky, receiving tutoring in the writings of Karl Marx. But, Ho Chi Minh's thirst for glimpses of more of the world led him next to the Republic of China, controlled by Chiang Kai-shek and the nationalists. He hurried back to Moscow in 1927, however, when Chiang's agents attacked suspected communists. Ho's odyssey continued to Paris, Thailand, and the British colony of Hong Kong where he was jailed after organizing the Indochinese Communist Party in 1929. Released from jail, Ho spent the 1930s practicing the Marxist lessons he had learned in Moscow, operating from a base just inside China and, as he calmly described it, "devoted solely to his national family." World events were moving even more rapidly than the world traveler, and in 1938, dictators were flexing their muscles.

In 1938, Germany's Adolf Hitler marched into Sudetenland and met in Munich with Great Britain's Prime Minister Neville Chamberlain to discuss the future of the rest of Czechoslovakia. Earlier that year, the Nazi leader had annexed Austria. Italy's Benito Mussolini had overwhelmed Ethiopia three years earlier as the impotent League of Nations stood on the sidelines, professing shock and displeasure. Japan's military had been brutally making its way across China since 1931, raping and pillaging while serving an emperor who considered himself divine. Thus, Chamberlain, fearing another world war, naively appeased Hitler in Munich, allowing the Germans to move into the remainder of Czechoslovakia. The Nazis would be far from satisfied, proceeding in September 1939 into Poland, which he divided with the Soviet Union's Stalin, igniting World War II as Great Britain and France rallied around doomed Poland. Mussolini attacked Albania that year, and Hitler in 1940 turned his attention to the Netherlands, Belgium, and France. Japan, allied with Germany and Italy, focused its military might on China, committing heinous atrocities on civilians, and Ho watched as much of the world became engulfed by the war's flames.

Germany quickly by-passed the Maginot Line, the defensive perimeter which had been constructed after the Great War as security against further German aggression, and took aim at France. Still operating from a safe haven just inside China, Ho perhaps viewed the six week war which saw France fall to the Nazis as an opportunity to liberate Vietnam. As we know, Hitler had other intentions. When France surrendered in June 1940, the Germans turned administration of the natural resources of Indochina over to Hitler's Vichy government, led by Marshall Henri Petain, a World War I hero. The natural products of Vietnam, especially rubber, coal, and oil were invaluable to Hitler and his Italian and Japanese friends as they continued to eye additional prey. Ho, sensing that his goal of national liberation needed to be launched from within Vietnam formed the Viet Minh in 1941 with Vo Nguyen Giap and Pham Van Dung. It should be noted that this trio of communists saw their objective as an independent Vietnam. As the war became even bigger, they cooperated with the western nations who by the time of Ho's return to his homeland in 1941 included Great Britain, the Free French resistance, Chiang Kai-shek's Republic of China, the Soviet Union which had been invaded by Hitler in the summer of that year, and the United States which had been attacked by Imperial Japan at Pearl Harbor in December 1941. Always, Ho's plan focused on the independence of Vietnam, occupied in 1941 by Marshall Petain's pro-Nazi Vichy government with Japanese military assistance. Ho listened closely to what President Franklin Roosevelt said about colonial self-determination.

The American president was an ideological disciple of Woodrow Wilson, in whose administration he had served as assistant secretary of the navy. Since his privileged childhood, FDR had traveled the globe. Roosevelt understood America's own struggle for independence and was opposed to colonial powers such as Great Britain and France re-claiming their foreign territories after the war's conclusion. Complicating his Wilsonian belief in self-determination was his need to first win the war by cooperating with Great Britain's Prime Minister Winston Churchill and the leader of the Free French, General Charles De Gaulle. Roosevelt once described himself to his close friend, Secretary of the Treasury Henry Morganthau as "a juggler." He skillfully moved forward in the European Theater by placating Churchill, who wanted to hold on to India, and De Gaulle, who wished to see France become great again after Hitler was defeated. The "juggler" needed to work closely with Stalin whose populace had paid a tremendous price on the Eastern Front. Roosevelt wished to bring ththe Soviet Union into the war against Japan, which was fighting with tenacity in the Pacific Theater. Domestic politics was always being juggled. Roosevelt won an unprecedented third term in 1940 and prepared for another election as 1944 approached. Indochina became a sideshow of sorts; the president understood the need to help secure colonial independence, the moral correctness of that goal, but the big war was more of a priority. Ending colonialism could wait until victory, the commander-in-chief believed. The pages of history are littered with the debris of missed opportunities and good intensions.

Ho and his Viet Minh worked with Chiang's government to sabotage the Vichy forces and to launch guerilla attacks against the Japanese. He became known to the Americans as a result of his aid in rescuing downed pilots, freeing captives, and using the Viet Minh to harass the enemy. In Ho's judgment, by helping the Americans he could secure independence for Vietnam. He understood the word "independence" from his earlier study of the American Revolution and his on-site tour. The presence of American agents in Vietnam starting in 1942 appealed to Ho Chi Minh because the Office of Strategic Services (OSS) represented Franklin Roosevelt who Ho believed would help Vietnam ultimately win its independence. FDR had told Winston Churchill before Pearl Harbor when the two leaders signed the Atlantic Charter that he was supportive of colonial self-government. In 1943, the American president had told his son, Elliott, that he was opposed to "further French imperialistic ambitions." He bluntly told the British the following year that France had "milked it (Indochina) for one hundred years" and the Vietnamese people were "worse off than they were at the beginning." He grasped the unfairness of European domination.

Roosevelt's declining health resulting from polio and high blood pressure did not sidetrack his 1944 re-election bid, but he appeared to realize that freeing colonies from greedy European nations would be a process which could take a generation. Change comes slowly. As he commenced his final few months of life, he explored giving Vietnam to China, but Chiang, understanding his country's previous experience in the area declined. Chiang worried about assimilation. In January 1945, FDR told Secretary of State Edward R. Stettinius, "I still do not want to get mixed up in any Indochina decision...action at this time is premature." A war must be won. The OSS' William Donovan agreed. Heading to Yalta the next month for what would be his last conference with Stalin and Churchill, the president was focused on securing the Soviet Union's help in the Pacific against the Japanese and destroying Fascism. Within two months, Roosevelt would be dead, felled by a cerebral hemorrhage in April 1945. In Vietnam, Ho and the Viet Minh continued to assist the OSS.

The exploits of the OSS' Deer Team in 1945 is significant because Ho and Giap were key players. Helping OSS operatives rescue imprisoned American airmen was perilous, but the actions of the Viet Minh helped divert Japanese attention. Parachuting into Vietnam, the OSS forces were greeted by Viet Minh. Ho told them he hoped Vietnam would receive a boost toward independence similar to the Philippines. He entrusted the Deer Team's Major Archimedes L. A. Patti with a letter to America's new president, Harry Truman, which re-affirmed Ho's commitment to a Declaration of Independence for Vietnam. The correspondence was similar to the document which Ho had attempted to present Woodrow Wilson at the 1919 Paris Peace Conference. He stressed that nationalism and self-determination were his motivation. Again, he received no response from our chief executive, Harry Truman,who in August 1945 was unleashing the Atomic Bomb on Japan. Ho was granted an audience with General Claire Chennault who was coordinating the rescue efforts of the Deer Team from a base in Kuming, China. Ho requested, and received, an au-tographed photo of Chennault, which Ho believed elevated his status. The Free French warned that Ho was "sly, clever, powerful, deceptive, ruthless-and deadly." Ho discovered that one of the Deer Team members was a French spy, and he secured his prompt replacement. Ill, Ho was treated by an American medic, Paul Hoagland, for malaria and dysentery and prom-ised to continue helping the OSS gather intelligence.

On August 16, Ho read his Declaration of Independence in Hanoi and proclaimed the Democratic Republic of Vietnam. Ten days later, Emperor Bao Dai, who had been used as a figurehead by the Vichy government and the Japanese military, abdicated and warned the French about trying to re-establish colonialism in Indochina. The association between the OSS and the Viet Minh continued into September 1945 as Ho assisted in freeing 136 American prisoners of war and ascertained the fate of pilots missing in action. He stressed to the Deer Team that nationalism-not communism-was his goal for Vietnam's future. Late that month, however, the OSS' Lieutenant A Peter Dewey had mixed feelings about the future. By then, Truman had detonated two atomic bombs, and the Imperial Empire had surrendered on the deck of the <u>USS Missouri</u>. Dewey, well-connected politically in the United States with an ex-congressman father and his relative presidential hopeful Thomas Dewey, said as he prepared to leave Saigon, "Cochinchina is burning, the French and British are finished here and we ought to clear out of Southeast Asia." Taking his own advice, Dewey headed to the airport after meeting with two journalists when a group of Viet Minh, mistaking him for a French officer because his jeep flew no American flags, was ambushed and killed, shot in the head. Both France and the Viet Minh blamed each other.

British commander General D.D. Gracey had forbidden the flying of flags except by himself. Chaos ruled in Vietnam with armed Japanese soldiers still around, French nationals released from prisons, disgraced Vichy roaming the streets, General Gracey trying to maintain order, and the Deer Team trying to sort out the true loyalty of Ho and Giap. Ho had admitted his communist ties to a member of the Deer Team and asked, "Can't we be friends?" Another team member had reviewed Ho's wording of his draft of the Declaration of Independence which included familiar words: "All the peoples of the earth are equal from birth, all the peoples have a right to live, to be happy and free...." The frustration and confusion permeating Vietnam in September 1945 was evident in Dewey's final comments about the Viet Minh: "It's the French they're after. Not us, nor even the British." But in the autumn of 1945, after months of working closely with Ho and the Viet Minh, Peter Dewey, an OSS agent, became the first American killed in what would become America's longest war. His name is omitted from the Vietnam Veterans Memorial. The Second World War had ended in September 1945, and another conflict commenced. Ho's dream of independence, Vietnamese-style, was shattered as President Harry Truman turned Vietnam over to Charles De Gaulle and the new French government which wished to use Indochina and its natural riches to regain its grandeur as long as the United States footed the bills. This time the war would be against communists, and Ho Chi Minh, by his own admission qualified as one of those in this new Cold War.

THE DOUBLE-EDGED SWORD

"We did not choose to be the guardian at the gate. But there is no one else."
—Lyndon Johnson, 1966

O NE OF THE creatures which roams through the history of the Cold war is the beast of American exceptionalism. As I survey our nation's past, I always emphasize to students that America was populated by people who arrived under duress: hungry and desperate people who walked across an Asian land bridge thousands of years ago, religious dissenters on vessels such as the *Mayflower* in 1620 who fled persecution back home, Scotch-Irish Presbyterians who detested the Church of England, French Huguenots who were oppressed by Roman Catholics, Roman Catholics oppressed by an Anglican government, debtors just released from jail, second sons wishing to escape the favoritism of primogeniture, aspiring entrepreneurs, dreamers who believed this was a land of liberty and equality, bold risk-takers and adventurers, and African slaves sold into bondage to harvest the labor-intensive crops of the South. All of these first Americans came under duress.

Our national identity was molded by the aforementioned people and those who came after them commencing in the 1880s, New Immigrants arrived in New York City from places like Poland and Greece searching for opportunities which Old Europe denied them, often because of their religion or social class or ethnicity. The New Immigrants, the huddled masses tempest-tossed of Emma Lazarus' Statue of Liberty, washed ashore at

Ellis Island, searching for the golden door. This mix of people who arrived under duress, with their backs against the wall, in a sense, and the New Immigrants who appeared later with oddly spelled names and unusual religions, built, through the sweat of their brows, literally, the United States. Include the Chinese workers who constructed the railroads of California. We are a nation of immigrants who have accomplished much in a relatively brief period of time.

Some of our forebears succeeded, scrambling up the ladder of economic success; many did not, ground up by the hardships of industrialization. It should be noted that industrialism and calls for our Manifest Destiny produced a jagged edge to our national fabric. Always, we moved about the continent, mastering the land and subduing any population which stood in the way: Native Americans, Mexicans, for instance. Over time, we evolved into backseat drivers, of sorts. We were insecure because of our humble origins, and we wished to demonstrate to the rest of the world our success. America is a cocky, impatient, materialistic, and aggressive place. Therefore, despite the presence of a sizable number of Loyalists in the British colonies on the eve of the Revolution, Jefferson, Adams, and the other Founding Fathers would convince everyone of the righteousness of our cause. No one should dare object or resist. We were driven by an almost missionary zeal that we were a chosen, exceptional people. Over time, this became national dogma, celebrated each July 4th with fireworks, parades, and speeches. Organizations such as the Colonial Dames and the Daughters of the American Revolution, proud of their brave and patriotic ancestors, illustrate this national trait. But our cocky self-assuredness bordered on arrogance, created enemies around the world. Our success in so many sectors, economic, scientific, technological, material, military affairs has become a double-edged sword.

In the twentieth century, as we have seen, it was Woodrow Wilson, the scholar son of a Presbyterian minister, who wished to first win the

Great War as an Associated Power of the Allies (notice, we were different) and then to preside over the 1919 Paris Peace Conference, much as he had dominated his Princeton University classroom, and make the world safe for democracy. His superior intellect, his Presbyterian predestination, and his believe in American exceptionalism would rule in Versailles, he thought. In Paris in 1919, however, the brilliant Dr. Wilson, president of an exceptional nation of immigrants, received a practical education at the hands of France's Georges Clemenceau, who had encountered German militarism earlier in 1870-1871 and wished to neuter Germany so it would never again be a threat to France or any other nation. The memories of the Franco-Prussian War, not Wilsonian platitudes about "self-determination," dominated the conference. He ignored Ho Chi Minh's pleas. The older nations had long ago abandoned idealism and replaced it with harsh realism. As we know, Woodrow Wilson did secure his League of Nations, which he believed would mature into an organization of international peacekeeping. His international forum with himself, of course, at the helm would be shattered, first by America's isolationism in the 1920s and 1930s and then by the international demons who came to power after World War I. A sequel, a much more deadly conflict, erupted. This situation, compounded by the worldwide Great Depression, faced Franklin Roosevelt who, as I have asserted, tried to cling to dreams of self-determination of peoples, one of his mentor's Fourteen Points.

American exceptionalism, that double-edged sword, is part of our collective DNA. President Lyndon B. Johnson, a gifted young protégée of Roosevelt, liked to speak of gallant ancestors who fought at the Alamo and the Battle of San Jacinto, ancestors who, interestingly, were absent from both Mexican War clashes. We are the descendants of what Thomas Jefferson called "demigods," exceptional people imbued with "the Spirit of '76." In Vietnam, however, we misunderstood the history of unjust French colonialism. We thought of ourselves as the sole legitimate guardians of democracy and the ideals of the Revolution. Therefore, anyone who seemed unlike us became suspect; no one else, as Johnson with his fictionalized ancestors believed, had the power. Our brand was the only brand. We were the parent.

In 1945, as a Cold War began between us and the Soviet Union, we mistakenly were convinced that self-determination for Vietnam could only occur under French tutelage and only on a schedule developed by France. So what if it took time to implement? That strategy would prevent Vietnam from entering Moscow's orbit, we believed. The mistake we made at that key moment was not sensing the unfairness of colonialism, despite the fact we had experienced it ourselves. WE were the world's superpower in 1945. WE had nuclear weapons. France was OUR friend in the Cold War. And in our view, Ho Chi Minh, Vietnamese communist, had no role to play in our plan for winning that war. He would just have to step aside, even if Vietnam was his country.

A FORMULA FOR CATASTROPHE

"They (the Americans) are only interested in replacing the French...."
—Ho Chi Minh, 1945

THE PATERNALISTIC ATTITUDE of France toward Vietnam, similar to that
displayed by our own Mother Country toward us prior to the American
Revolution, resumed in 1945 with one official pledging that it was time for
"the Annamite beggars" to resume their subservient position as a French colony. Since the time of exploration of the Mekong River and Roman Catholic
missionaries, France has administered Vietnam as a place rich with coal,
spices, rice, and rubber occupied by a docile population. It was a hunter's
paradise and recreational haven for visiting members of the wealthy French
leisure class. Ho's Viet Minh argued that the natives, just like anyone, wanted independence. Surely, a country which had endured the experience of
being a British colony could understand such things. As we have seen, Ho
used Thomas Jefferson's Declaration of Independence as a guide to self-government, seasoned with communist ideology. Rebuffed by Washington in
the first days of the Truman Administration despite his friendship with the
OSS, Ho turned to the Soviet Union, where he had studied two decades
earlier. And, after the 1949 Chinese Revolution which drove Chiang off the
mainland and brought communist Mao Zedong to power, Ho used aid from
China to bolster his Viet Minh. I contend that Ho Chi Minh had communist proclivities most of his life, but he wanted independence more than

Marxism. Additionally, I suggest that Ho was somewhat wary of China because of Vietnam's earlier experience with Chinese occupiers.

Part of the problem Ho faced after the defeat of Japan and the other Axis Powers in 1945 was the credibility France had lost when Adolph Hitler had easily conquered France in the summer of 1940. De Gaulle believed that now he could demonstrate to the world the resurgence of a true French Empire –as opposed to that of the pro-Nazi Vichy government on the compliant backs of native people in Africa and Southeast Africa. France, 1945, was a NEW France. If he had lived, perhaps Franklin Roosevelt, the juggler, could have out maneuvered De Gaulle and the British, who were attempting to re-assert themselves in India. That, too, would fail with Indian independence. Roosevelt expressed his position in a document included in the *Pentagon Papers,* a detailed and disturbing study of America's descent into the Vietnamese quagmire. Roosevelt noted that he had explained to Churchill's ambassador Lord Fairfax in early 1944, "I had, for over a year expressed the opinion that Indo-china (sic) should not go back to France but that it should be administered by an international trusteeship. France has had the country-thirty million inhabitants for nearly one hundred years, and the people are worse off than they were at the beginning." Summing up his viewpoint, FDR added, "The people of Indo-china are entitled to something better than that."

FDRs analysis of the situation in Indochina was ancient history by 1946. Harry Truman, of course, did not have Roosevelt's extensive foreign policy experience. He, furthermore, lacked his predecessor's political skills. When Churchill gave his Westminster College address in 1946 warning the world of an Iron Curtain descending on Eastern Europe, the battle lines of the Cold War were clearly being formed. Vietnam needed to remain under the control of the West. So, the Truman Administration, scrambling to prevent the extension of the Iron Curtain into Southeast Asia, supported the return of France as a colonial power, which came with 35,000 French troops. In

March 1946, less than a year after FDRs death, France announced Vietnam would be a "free state within the French Union." That was a clear announcement that the new boss would be the same as the old boss. The devil was in the details; there was considerable fine print.

Ho travelled to Paris to argue his case but was largely ignored. The only positive part of the "free state within the French Union" arrangement was that China, under Chiang until 1949, withdrew from Vietnam. Ho explained this development clearly, "The last time the Chinese came they stayed a thousand years." Accepting the reality of Indochina, circa 1946, Ho observed, "I prefer to sniff French shit for five years than eat Chinese shit for the rest of my life." By the end of the year, Viet Minh battled French in Hanoi, organizing small units which probed for weaknesses in their colonial overseers. Initially, Joseph Stalin paid little attention to Indochina. His ambitions were in Eastern Europe, seeking to secure the Iron Curtain. Truman surrounded himself with advisors who failed to grasp the intricacies of communism. To them, communism was monolithic, spewing forth from Moscow, and must be resisted vigorously by the West. To these policymakers, French colonialism was preferable to seeing Ho in charge of the natural bounty of Vietnam.

Truman's first secretary of state, James F. Byrnes, was definitely a Cold Warrior. He saw the Iron Curtain as more of a mesh which threatened the entire world, and in the early months of the Truman Administration reminded the Soviets of the awesome power of our nuclear arsenal. One of Byrnes' successors was Dean Acheson who surmised in 1947, "The question whether Ho was as much a nationalist as Communist" was irrelevant because "all Stalinists in colonial areas are nationalists." Thus, the United States, an exceptional nation which understood the threat to democracy better than anyone else, was going to support France; there would be no self-determination for Vietnam. Stalin would not be allowed to wrap his Iron Curtain, or mesh, around Southeast Asia. Case closed.

That year, the state department's George F. Kennan, writing as Mister X in *Foreign Affairs* penned an 8000-word defense of what came to be known as "containment," the rationale for fighting communism on all fronts. Kennan argued that Stalin and his comrades were motivated by "the traditional and instinctive Russian sense of insecurity." The American diplomat commented that two world wars, the 1917 Russian Revolution which installed the Bolsheviks, and the rise of a totalitarian state under V.I. Lenin and Joseph Stalin combined to produce a dictatorship where a bold communist power "moves inexorably along a prescribed path, like a toy automobile wound up and headed in a given direction, stopping only when it meets some unanswerable force." The mission of the United States in the Cold War was to become that force, defending "the interests of a peaceful and stable world," Kennan explained. That was our destiny, 1947. We must be prepared to expend resources to "contain" the threat.

American cash would be dispensed to prevent a Red Tide from spreading across the world. The $400,000,000 Truman Doctrine boosted noncommunist elements in Greece and Turkey. It demonstrated our willingness to open our pocketbooks to deny Soviet encroachment. Byrnes' immediate successor, General George C. Marshall, explained at the 1947 Harvard University commencement that billions of dollars in economic credits would be spent to help war-shattered Europe rebuild and resist the panacea offered by communism. This Marshall Plan was an attempt to deny Stalin allies in Western Europe. Our Cold War activities went far beyond solely economic aid. The Central Intelligence Agency rose from the ashes of the OSS (which Truman disliked) in 1948, serving as an international network of vigilant intelligence agents keeping tabs on our foes. The founding in 1949 of the North Atlantic Treaty Organization (NATO) was further evidence of America and its friends trying to contain communism.

That year, the Soviet Union announced the detonation of an atomic bomb in Kazakhstan. Now, we would need to pause before brandishing our nuclear arsenal at Stalin. Later that year, Mao's Chinese communists defeated Chiang, who fled to Taiwan. The question whispered around America was: "Who lost China?" Truman, the underdog, had defeated Republican Thomas Dewey, Dixiecrat Strom Thurmond, and Progressive Henry Wallace (who had been one of FDRs vice presidents) in the 1948 presidential campaign. But, now, just a few months later we found out Stalin had nuclear weapons and Mao had China. America had a case of buyer's remorse. "Who lost China?" Indeed.

Truman, who certainly lacked Roosevelt's commitment to liberating the colonies of allies, wanted to avoid antagonizing France, especially at this critical time. For several years, the president had been flying in supplies to French forces in Vietnam. Now, American aid dramatically increased, proving to Ho Chi Minh that the vapors of independence which once perfumed the corridors of Washington had been extinguished. The administration's George C. Marshall was blunt: "We have fully recognized France's sovereign position in that area." Re-installed, Emperor Bao Dai lacked credibility with the Vietnamese people; his regime was French sponsored with the Europeans controlling the country's defense, domestic affairs, and finances. Ho vigorously contended that he was not an acolyte of the Soviet Union, but he was ignored by the Truman Administration. After all, as the decade of the 1940s concluded, the Soviets had the atomic bomb and Mao had driven Chiang off the mainland. To the United States, Ho, despite his protests, must be part of the international communism web which threatened democracy.

In 1949, Truman supported Secretary of State Dean Acheson's request for $15,000,000 in assistance for France's resurrected empire in Indochina. To the Americans as the first decade of the Cold War ended, Ho was a Soviet agent, intent on challenging a western ally. Was this not clear? The catastrophe which loomed for France, however, was fueled by political instability in the general assembly and the war-weariness of the French people, far more than a perceived threat by Ho Chi Minh to democracy. France was still trying to rebuild after the devastation of World War II and the tarnished reputation of pro-Nazi Vichy France.

During our own revolution, George Washington was aided by British debt from the Seven Years' War and questions in Great Britain about how a lengthy war against colonists who did not fight by the traditional rules of the battlefield might affect morale in England. Similarly, Ho's promise of independence to his people could achieve victory by the Viet Minh driving up the financial cost of France's Asian *grandeur* to the Americans and to the French populace. Furthermore, the Viet Minh terrorized the enemy and then faded into the countryside. "Who were these revolutionaries?" Paris and Washington might inquire. And, "How much money will be required to subdue them?" Ho believed time was definitely on his side.

Briefly in 1950, some in our state department entertained thoughts that Ho might not be "a Soviet surrogate," But Dean Acheson summed up Ho's political allegiance by explaining he was a "Chi Commie hatchet man...." Agreeing was Undersecretary of State Dean Rusk, who would himself become embroiled in the Vietnam conflict in little more than a decade. Appearing in 1950 before the Senate Foreign Relations Committee, Rusk explained that, "Ho Chi Minh is tied in with the (Soviet) Politburo, our policy is to support Bao Dai and the French in Indochina until we have time to help them establish a going concern." So, France took millions of dollars in aid from the United States, ignored Emperor Bao Dai (who spent his time at European casinos and with courtesans), underestimated Ho Chi Minh's strength among the people of Vietnam, and expended its military's blood.

By the summer of 1950, communist forces had overrun the Korean peninsula with weapons from Stalin and troops from Mao. Truman found himself mobilizing a United Nations contingent to re-establish the border in Korea between communist Kim Il Sung and our ally, Syngman Rhee. In the Cold War, we were cast, in Lyndon Johnson's words, as "the guardian." This bold act of communist aggression settled the question. The Soviet Union and China were intent on bathing the world in blood. We had countered Moscow in Greece and Turkey with the Truman Doctrine and strengthened capitalism in Europe with the Marshal Plan. Our CIA and NATO monitored the enemy's movements. But now they had the atomic bomb and the most populous nation on earth and were trying to conquer Korea. Additionally, the communists had formed the Warsaw Pact as a combined military in Eastern Europe, a counter to NATO.

It seemed to us that Ho, despite his earlier friendship with the Deer Team and his comments about his nationalist intentions, was merely another tool of monolithic communism. With Wisconsin Senator Joseph McCarthy warning that 205 communists had infiltrated the Truman State Department, our beleaguered president saw France, colonial France, as our bulwark in Asia against the Viet Minh. We know that the 1950-1953 Korean police action would further ensnare the United States in foreign wars because of our visibility at the United Nations. Since France seemed determined to hold on to Indochina, we would stand with them. As France explained to us in the midst of the Korean conflict, if we failed to support them in Vietnam, next to fall would be the Middle East and Africa. One American official, R. Allen Griffith, expressed alarm: "(The Bao Dai government) has no grass roots. It therefore has no appeal whatsoever to the masses." Griffith's cautious voice was an isolated one as our monetary commitment to maintaining France's colony increased, even as that country by 1952 suffered 90,000 casualties in what the French people termed *la sale guerre,* "the dirty war." No one would have predicted that Vietnam would become, for many Americans, a *la sale guerre* a decade later.

THE END OF THE FIRST ACT

"Now we can see it clearly-like light at the end of a tunnel."
—General Henri Navarre, 1953

THE 1952 PRESIDENTIAL election brought to the White House a legend-ary World War II hero, Dwight D. Eisenhower. As a military man, "Ike" understood the importance of having a clear strategy as well as the costs of battle. His leadership of the supreme allied command, dealing with egotistical fellow generals and meddlesome politicians, had produced vic-tory in Europe. The June 6, 1944 D Day invasion of Nazi-held France was a tactical masterpiece: 160,000 American, British, and Canadian troops coming ashore at dawn in Normandy along a fifty mile stretch of beach. Eisenhower was prepared on D Day for failure, even drafting a memo-randum taking responsibility if the offensive had not succeeded. D Day, however, as the world saw, was a masterful success. Parachutes and glid-ers descending behind Nazi lines, and the soldiers of the Allied nations advancing into France. "Ike," nonetheless, was not a government figure, even though Franklin Roosevelt had catapulted him over more experienced generals. Eisenhower was a statistical and logistical wizard; he understood risks and probability.

By 1952, the Korean police action helped convince Eisenhower that his talents could be of use once more. Not partisan, he had been courted by both political parties, and he became a Republican. It was almost like he flipped a coin to determine his party. He decided his nation needed him as commander-in-chief, and as he pledged in 1952, "I will go to Korea," the voters saluted. Before inauguration day, he had visited the Korean peninsula, grasping the intricacies and dangers of war on the Asian mainland, especially close to Mao's China, with its teeming population.

The new American president feared another Asian conflict in Indochina, perhaps ensnaring the United States. All through the Truman years, France had projected itself as the western country which could prevent a communist takeover of Southeast Asia. As we have seen, Truman's Cold Warriors were willing to bankroll the colonial power. One after another, they had made their minds up about Ho. By 1952, we were even providing Emperor Bao Dai with an annual allowance of $4,000,000 which he placed in French and Swiss banks. The Viet Minh's small bands of guerrillas attacked French garrisons, and the war became increasingly unpopular among the French people, who saw it as endless.

While there was an armistice in Korea as the Eisenhower presidency began in 1953, the new president detected no enthusiasm for his proposal to let the United Nations broker peace in Vietnam. His secretary of state, John Foster Dulles, was as steadfast as the foreign policy advisors to the previous administration and offered France $500,000,000 to continue its efforts against the Viet Minh. Containment began to look more like roll back, and its costs to France in men and to the United States in dollars were escalating. Dulles explained his support of meeting the challenge of Ho Chi Minh this way, "For all his claims of independence, Ho was essentially reliant on his Communist patrons, who did not hesitate to subvert his goals to advance their own interests." These interests were to topple Indochina, and like a row of dominoes nations in Asia would fall one after one to Moscow. This Domino Theory became the mantra for Dulles, and he pushed Eisenhower to support France's costly efforts against the communists.

Interestingly, there is some evidence that Mao's Chinese believed in 1953 that the French would abandon their Asian colony. Additionally, relations between the Soviet Union and the people's Republic of China were not always cordial, even after Joseph Stalin's death the year. One of the missed signals of the Cold War is the rivalry in the international communist movement. But the French, trying to lay to rest the corpse of Vichy, did not wish to appear weak in Vietnam, as they had been when the Nazis conquered Paris. Therefore, the French commander, General Henri Navarre, made it clear that his country had no intention of abandoning Indochina. The western world depended on the French to stand firm against the Red Tide, to roll it back in Vietnam. Navarre and other French generals visited the United States, warning Congress about the dangers of falling dominoes. He planned to confront the Viet Minh at Dien Bien Phu near the Laotian border: "Now we can see it clearly-like light at the end of the tunnel." Some French, who were more experienced about the region, warned that a battle in the valley around Dien Bien Phu would turn into "a meat grinder." To Navarre, cocky and perhaps believing the Americans would come to his aid if necessary, with atomic weapons, believed the French base in the valley was secure. Viet Minh General Giap saw it differently: "We decided to wipe out at all costs the whole enemy force at Dien Bien Phu." To the French, this battle would be a perfect opportunity to demolish the Viet Minh, who seemed to prefer small unit attacks, and, surely, Navarre reasoned, the communists could not use the hills surrounding the valley as bases for an artillery assault.

In the early months of the Eisenhower administration, Dulles and others promoted the view that all communists took their orders from Moscow. Again, contrary views were swept away, even when accompanied by indisputable facts. Yugoslavia's Marshal Tito stands as a classic example of the cracks in the communist monolith. Additionally, Mao's China had endured considerable casualties fighting the United Nations' coalition in Korea, and Mao saw the People's Republic of China-not the Soviet Union-as the primary example of Marxist revolution, especially in Asia.

Ho and Giap, long over their flirtation with America, realized that Chinese weapons, hidden in the hills, and Viet Minh cadres could extinguish Navarre's "light at the end of the tunnel" at Dien Bien Phu. As we have seen, the Viet Minh leadership, undoubtedly, were communist with a sprinkling of nationalism; opinions will vary concerning this combination and let us not be naïve about them. Even when the two worked with the Deer Team, they had not attempted to hide their ideology. Ho Chi Minh had always acknowledged his leanings; he had studied Marxism in Moscow in the 1920s and 1930s, even avoiding Stalin's purges. But his overall goal remained constant through the years; he wanted Vietnam to achieve its own brand of self-determination, free of colonialism. He had been rejected by the United States, first at the 1919 Paris peace Conference and then in 1945 when the Truman administration backed the return of France's Asian empire. The future of colonialism would be at stake in the valley of Dien Bien Phu for fifty-six days when the French arrived in December 1953. The siege turned out to be France's last stand. Furthermore, it would provide Ho a clear answer to his question to the Deer Team nearly a decade earlier: "Can we still be friends?" We would, as Ho suspected, succeed France, if it failed in the valley.

Under General Navarre, his army in the valley would be a combination of French soldiers, Foreign Legionnaires (mostly German), North Africans, and Asian loyalists (perhaps comprising half of the colonial contingent). On the other hand, the Viet Minh used distaste for a century of French colonialism with its, as FDR aptly called it, "milking," and the promise of independence, albeit communist, to dominate and terrorize the countryside. He recruited troops from around the area. Giap proved to be an outstanding tactician. If France wished for a "winner takes all" battle, his Viet Minh would be ready. Using Chinese and Soviet artillery hidden in the hills around Dien Bien Phu, he trapped the French in their base. For nearly two months, the Viet Minh dug tunnels to French outposts, then raining death down on the enemy from artillery. American aircraft supplied the French with airdrops, but hostile weather restricted this aid. And those in Washington, Like

John Foster Dulles, who entertained the possibility of using atomic weapons (Dulles estimated three) to break the siege were rebuffed by Eisenhower. As a military man, "Ike" had witnessed the effects of war which could easily spread. In combat, anything could transpire. He had inherited Korea, where Mao in 1951 had sent human waves against United Nations' commander Douglas MacArthur.

Eisenhower in 1954 did not want another land war in Asia with American troops playing an increased role. Despite being somewhat non-partisan, he also understood that American public support for such a venture would quickly become unpopular in congress-just as it had for the French people. According to aide Sherman Adams, Eisenhower did not want "total war with Red China…." The joint chiefs of staff agreed and told the president, "Indochina is devoid of decisive military objectives…." Was this the ideal location for America to fight the Cold War? What, really, would we gain? Our ally Great Britain was again led by Winston Churchill, who in 1954 had learned something painful about nationalism's potency in India. Churchill signaled "Ike" that his country would not be part of any attempt to salvage the besieged French at Dien Bien Phu.

On May 7, 1954, General Giap raised the red flag over France's command bunker in the valley. Eisenhower, relieved that he had not been lured further into the conflict, appears to have become philosophical about the situation in Indochina: "The most you can work out is a practical way of getting along." While not especially eloquent, that became the American position as victors and losers met in Geneva to discuss the region's future. At the Geneva Conference, it was agreed among the Soviet Union, China, France, Great Britain, the Viet Minh, the Associated States of Indochina, and the United States that within two years an election would be held to determine the political make-up in Vietnam. A dividing line, supposedly temporary, was established at the 17th parallel as everyone awaited United Nations' supervised elections which never transpired. Roman Catholic Ngo Dinh Diem was installed in Saigon as president of the southern part of Vietnam, and 1.000,000 Roman Catholics from the north headed to South Vietnam. There is some research, interestingly, that the Viet Minh wished to prevent the establishment of a communist police state. The Chinese and Soviets accepted the 1954 partition and the promise of an election within two years, perhaps realizing that, over time, the communists wound dominate both sections of Vietnam. The French were bitter, believing that our country had interfered too much and helped too little as it lost its Asian colony. The new president of South Vietnam, Diem, saw the decisions made at Geneva differently. According to two scholars, he "understood that France's defeat (by the Nazis) in 1940 meant that colonialism was over in Southeast Asia." He brought along with him to power in Saigon his two brothers, one a Roman Catholic bishop and the other married to the divisive Madame Nhu (who described protesting Buddhists who immolated themselves in Saigon's thoroughfares in 1963 "a barbecue"). Another brother had been buried alive by the Viet Minh. The Diem brothers and Madame Nhu forced Emperor Bao Dai into exile within a year.

For the United States, it was still unclear what strategic importance South Vietnam offered. As an exceptional nation, we would sort through the wreckage of French colonialism. We understood the communist threat of the early years of the Cold War. Had we not displayed sound judgment in resisting the calls for nuclear weapons at Dien Bien Phu? And, Korea had taught us valuable lessons about being cautious in Asia. But, as I suggest, we had already made our first mistake in Vietnam: we had forgotten our own experience as a colony, and we had rejected Ho Chi Minh's earlier entreaties. Now, the West was in a Cold War against the evil of communism. France had failed in its mission, and the United States must step forward. With Ho in control of North Vietnam, we accepted a bigger role in what would morph into America's longest war, ultimately producing those names on that wall in Washington.

Immediately on September 8, 1954, we formed a new alliance, SEATO, the Southeast Asia Treaty Organization. It was comprised of the United States, Great Britain, France, Australia, New Zealand, the Philippines, Pakistan, Thailand, and the Associated States of Vietnam, Laos, and Cambodia. In this new organization, like in NATO, we were the senior partner. And was not NATO succeeding against communism in Europe? To Ho and Giap, the United States, had become the latest colonial power standing in their way of complete control of Vietnam. We are reminded of a decade earlier, when Ho had ominously warned France, "You can kill ten of my men for everyone I kill of yours but even at those odds, you will lose and I will win." Giap consistently spoke of the "final victory." These pledges were not merely boasts; they were made by people who are prepared to pay enormous costs to secure self-determination. America's first mistake in Vietnam was our disregard of lessons we should have learned in our own nation's struggle to be free of Great Britain's control in 1776. As we gathered at the Vietnam Veterans Memorial on a spring morning in 2000 to contemplate sacrifice, death, heroism, sacrifice, and duplicity, some of us realized that the mistakes commenced in 1945 and continued until communist tanks rolled into Saigon on April 30, 1975. Let us continue our analysis of the first error and what it created.

AUTOPSY

"Writing history, especially where it blends into current events, especially where that current event is Vietnam is a tremendous exercise."
—Leslie Gelb, *The Pentagon Papers,* 1969.

BY 1967, AMERICA's role in Vietnam had divided our nation, fracturing generations and families, and wrecking President Lyndon Johnson's dream of a Great Society, a wide-ranging assortment of projects like Head Start for low income and disabled preschoolers, VISTA, Volunteers In Service To America, a domestic Peace Corps, and Community Action Programs. The venom produced by the war poisoned social initiatives and robbed the chief executive of a progressive legacy. Vietnam was now about "commitment," promises that we had made to South Vietnam when it was established in 1954. The Texan was not about to cut and run away from this commitment, even if it destroyed his presidency and created hostilities within American families.

The United States Marines had come ashore at Da Nang in 1965, and outnumbered American soldiers had withstood a withering assault by waves of regular North Vietnamese troops that year at Ia Drang Valley. Johnson had secured congressional approval a year earlier for an expanded American presence as a response to the Gulf of Tonkin Incident, a questionable encounter between North Vietnamese patrol boats and two United States naval vessels. As the casualties increased, civil rights leader the Rev. Dr. Martin

Luther King, Jr. broke with President Johnson in 1967 and delivered his impassioned "A Time To Break Silence" speech, raising questions about the costs of our commitment which took valuable resources away from domestic programs. To many, it appeared the Vietnam War was the wrong war at the wrong place at the wrong time.

The conflict had become our first television war, dominating evening newscasts and morning headlines. The three television networks expanded their evening newscasts from fifteen to thirty minutes in order to air footage and commentary from clashes occurring thousands of miles away between the re-named communist Viet Cong and the South Vietnamese with their American allies. Thus, Secretary of Defense Robert S. McNamara commissioned in 1967 a top secret comprehensive study of America's involvement in Southeast Asia since the 1940s. This study was entitled officially "Report of the Office of the Secretary of Defense Vietnam Task Force," better known as *The Pentagon Papers.* The analysis was to answer a key question: "How did this happen?" This top-secret study was comprised of forty-eight boxes of material with 3000 pages of narrative and 4000 pages of supporting documents. The monumental project took eighteen months to complete, and by the time of its submission in January 1969, McNamara, like Lyndon Johnson, had become a casualty of the war. Assassinations of American leaders had damaged our nation: King in April 1968 and Senator Robert F. Kennedy two months later. Peace negotiations in Paris between the warring parties moved at a snail's pace. A communist offensive in early 1968 had been a military failure, but it had led nightly television newscasts. Over 500,000 American troops were stationed in Indochina, and every town in the United States had grieved for men killed in action in a faraway conflict which the president had promised in the 1964 campaign he would never expand. Therefore, Leslie Gelb presented *The Pentagon Papers* to then Secretary of Defense Clark Clifford on January 15, 1969, five days before the inauguration of President Richard M. Nixon who had pledged to "bring us together" by employing "a secret plan" for extricating America from the jungles and rice paddies of Vietnam.

One of the analysts who had waded through the sea of documents which chronicled decades of deceit at the highest levels of American government was Daniel Ellsberg, a former marine corps officer from 1954-1957. Once a proponent of the war, Ellsberg had reversed his opinions after considering our descent into the Vietnam quagmire. Ellsberg with accomplice Anthony Russo provided the *New York Times* with portions of *The Pentagon Papers* in 1971, igniting a First Amendment battle between the Nixon Administration and that newspaper which was decided in the press' favor by a 6-3 United States Supreme Court ruling, *New York Times Co. v. United States.* Other newspapers, *The Washington Post and The Boston Globe* also published excerpts of the study, and Alaska's anti-war Senator Mike Gravel read parts of the policy review aloud in a Senate subcommittee hearing. Copies of the study were published in paperback editions which could be obtained by the American public.

The Pentagon Papers and other primary sources released since 1971 tell a sad story of presidents and policymakers who had misled the public about progress of the war as it bled America and divided the nation. Roosevelt, as we have discussed, understood the complexities of colonialism, but he was focused on keeping his World War II coalition together. His successor, the inexperienced Harry Truman, was immediately confronted in 1945 by the Cold War and chose to bankroll France. The loss of China a few years later alarmed him and his advisors. Eisenhower, a military man, resisted calls for nuclear weapons at Dien Bien Phu, but he bought into the domino theory and increased America's military presence in Vietnam. They would, of course, only be "advisers," Eisenhower stressed. Kennedy, pledging to "go anywhere in the defense of liberty" when he was inaugurated in 1961 was definitely a cold warrior, as he wrestled with the Soviet Union's Nikita Khrushchev in Cuba and Berlin. Green Berets, special forces trained in a variety of skills, were sent to Vietnam from Fort Bragg. Johnson, the Texan, wanted to build a Great Society, but an increasingly unpopular war consumed him after the murky 1964 Gulf of Tonkin Incident. A consideration of these materials makes it clear that many mistakes were made by our leaders beginning in the 1940s, and the first one, as we have seen, was made in 1945 by our failure to take a different approach in Vietnam to colonialism.

Colonialism allowed European nations such as France, Great Britain, Germany, and Belgium to dominate huge regions of the world from Africa to the Middle East to South America to Asia. Colonies were often rich in natural resources like diamonds, oil, rice, gold, spices, coal, wild animals, and rubber. The colonies' soil was rich; the native peoples were not. By the early twentieth century colonialism was aging; its abuse of human rights could no longer be defended. One of the truisms of history is that people hunger for freedom to direct their own lives. As we have discussed, that was true in our own country during an earlier period. Unfair taxation, economic control, and social divisions by the Mother Country gave birth to the American Revolution. Certainly, those factors motivated Thomas Jefferson as he drafted our 1776 Declaration of Independence, with its inspiring words: "All men are created equal, they are endowed by their Creator with certain unalienable rights, among these are life, liberty, and the pursuit of happiness." Let us quickly note that Jefferson meant "all men" like himself and not women or people of color. I assert that these bold words were on Ho Chi Minh's mind from 1919 at the Paris Peace Conference and in 1945 when the Deer Team helped him prepare Vietnam's own Declaration of Independence, and even nurse him back to physical health. As domination of colonies by European countries in the 1940s eroded, we had an ideal opportunity to help Ho shape Vietnam's destiny. He was, indeed, a communist, but his nationalism was also tangible.

France's use of its Indochina colonies, especially Vietnam, as sources of income, natural resources, and hunting safaris for the elite lived on borrowed time in the 1940s. A mandarin class of natives, installed and guided by the French overseers was an easy target for the Viet Minh. Roman Catholics in a Buddhist region, enforcing unjust laws about land use and unjust payment to workers further strengthened Ho's hand. Self-determination is a potent force, impressing Woodrow Wilson and making its way into his 1918 Fourteen Points. His idealism hoped to re-make the post-Great War world and liberate colonies. That is why it appealed to the twenty-nine-year-old Ho Chi Minh in 1919. But, as we have seen, realism and revenge dominated the discussion at the Paris Peace Conference as France's Georges Clemenceau taught Dr. Woodrow Wilson a harsh lesson about the spoils of victory.

Within a generation hate flowed across the globe as Benito Mussolini engulfed Ethiopia and Albania. Japan, despite fighting on the victorious side in the Great War, became a military dictatorship. Adolph Hitler, forming an alliance with the aforementioned two, gobbled up *lebensraum* (living space) starting with Austria and then in 1938 Czechoslovakia. The world found itself ablaze again. When France fell in 1940 to the Nazis, its colony of Vietnam became the domain of the Vichy collaborators, with help from the Japanese military and the figurehead Emperor Bao Dai.

Bothered by colonialism, FDR, who had served in the Wilson administration, was a much more agile politician than academician Wilson. Roosevelt always looked to the future, a time when self-determination could occur. *The Pentagon Papers* begin with 1940. As we have found, the American president was determined to liberate Europe's colonies. His use of the word "milked" for Vietnam in 1944 is accurate. Since the 1800s, France had "milked" Indochina of taxes, labor, dignity, and natural resources.

The Viet Minh saw Roosevelt as a potential ally. On December 22, 1944, General Giap told a meeting of the Indochinese Communist Party (which he called "the organization"), "From Yugoslavia to China, countless numbers of people are struggling gloriously to win independence, freedom, and happiness. He urged his supporters to launch an armed struggle which would be bloody, but "We will advance, always advance until the day of liberation of the entire people."

The Pentagon Papers ask a key question early in the Study: "Ho Chi Minh: Asian Tito?" In their collaboration with the OSS' Deer Team in the last year of World War II, Ho and Giap demonstrated their loyalty to America in the search for downed pilots and prisoners held by the Japanese. Additionally, the "armed struggle" of the Viet Minh was invaluable in harassing the Japanese and Vichy government. The "organization," to use Giap's word, resisted the Japanese throughout 1945. When the Japanese broke away from the deteriorating Vichy bureaucrats, who were increasingly isolated after France was liberated by the allies, the communists proclaimed in March 1945, "The Japanese bandits will not liberate our people; on the contrary, they will increase oppression and exploitation." Shortly before his April death, Roosevelt re-iterated his position on the return of French colonialism in Vietnam, telling Charles Taussig that "he was concerned about the brown people in the East." The American president wanted France to concur "that independence was the ultimate goal."

Rapidly, much changed. The "juggler" died in Warm Springs, Georgia. Hitler and Mussolini met their ends. The Japanese were devastated by bombing and American military forces tightening the noose on the home islands. And the new president, Harry Truman, wished to keep France as a friend in the approaching Cold War, especially when De Gaulle raised the specter of communist encroachment. Truman chastised the Vichy elements for complicity with the Japanese military: "the French authorities cooperated with the Japanese and permitted them to enter and to effect military control of the colony." The Truman administration stated, "The interests of the United States are opposed to imperialism and favor progressive development, economically and politically, of dependent peoples until they are prepared for and are granted independence." Continuing, our state department stated its dilemma in the late spring of 1945: "The problem for the United States is whether it will be advisable, especially in view of the effect on United States global policies, to make demands on France in regard to Indochina...." We were quickly becoming the guardian of the Free World, a world which would have no room for an "Asian Tito."

First, Truman needed to ensure the capitulation of Japan (which occurred in Hiroshima and Nagasaki that August). He had to prepare for the Soviet Union's post-war ambitions. Giap was not in the mood to wait on Truman to dismantle France's colonial bureaucracy. The Viet Minh launched a general uprising on August 12. Giap reminded his followers that in 1940, "the French imperialists surrendered on bended knees and handed over our country to the invaders." Giap, like Ho, quoted from Thomas Jefferson's Declaration of Independence and listed grievances against France, much like Jefferson did in 1776. He asserted, "we shall from now on have no more connections with imperialist France...." As Japan formally surrendered on September 2, Ho and Giap again praised the United States as "a democratic country which has no territorial ambitions but has contributed particularly to the defeat of our enemy, Japanese fascism. Therefore, we regard the U.S. as a good friend."

The OSS was scrambling, trying to ascertain the true loyalties of the Viet Minh. On September 5-6, 1945, OSS Director William J. Donovan wrote a memorandum to Secretary of State James F. Byrnes describing the chaos ensuing in Indochina with defeated Japanese troops battling the Viet Minh and France eager to re-instate colonial control. Donovan stressed that the Viet Minh would resist any efforts by France or China (still controlled by Chiang) to turn the clock backwards. Donovan concluded his correspondence with prophetic words: "Trouble seems to be brewing and may break out after the armistice has been signed in Indochina." Later that month, Truman disbanded the OSS, eventually creating the Central Intelligence Agency.

As the last of the OSS presence evacuated Vietnam on September 17, the operatives recorded that they had said goodbye to their Vietnamese friends. Banners in every language, except French, proclaimed, "Welcome

Allies," "Welcome Peace Commission," "Down With French Imperialism," "Let's Kick Out French Imperialism," "Independence Or Death," "2,000,000 People Died Under French Domination," and "Vietminh For The Vietnamese." The American agents noted that their "friend of the forest," Ho Chi Minh was president of the provisional government since Bao Dai had abdicated, and "another friend of the forest," Vo Nguyen Giap ,was minister of the interior. In Washington, however, the decision had already been made, the mistake had already transpired, these two men were no longer our friends. The Cold War was underway, and France would have our endorsement until it was defeated in 1954 at Dien Bien Phu. Then, it would become our turn. All of this story is found in what I call the autopsy, better known as *The Pentagon Papers,* which made its way to the American public much too late.

IN RETROSPECT

"The greatest dangers of war seems to me not to be in the deliberate
actions of wicked men, but in the inability of harassed men to manage
events that have run away from them."
—Henry Kissinger, 1985

A FEW YEARS BEFORE the emotional 2000 ceremony at the Vietnam
Veterans Memorial, former Defense Secretary Robert McNamara, who
we will recall from the previous chapter, authorized *The Pentagon Papers* in
1967 published a *mea culpa* of sorts in 1995 entitled *In Retrospect*. McNamara,
one of John F. Kennedy's "best and brightest" came to Washington with
JFK in 1961 from a stellar but brief performance at Ford Motor Company.
He contributed to the broadening war left by Dwight Eisenhower and John
Foster Dulles, reducing the expanding conflict to charts and statistical anal-
yses. As an exceptional nation, we, obviously, were exceeding expectations
in Vietnam, McNamara advised Kennedy and Lyndon Johnson. Over time,
however, the deepening quicksand, worried McNamara, who evacuated the
Johnson Administration for the World Bank after setting in motion *The
Pentagon Papers,* which as we have seen digs deeply into the war's early years
and America's frenzy to defeat Ho Chi Minh.

Decades later, McNamara's *In Retrospect* appeared. Editorial page cartoonists had a field day ridiculing the book and its premise that the former defense secretary needed nearly thirty years to organize his thoughts.

Cartoonists use pens and wit like surgeons use scalpels, slicing into the subject at hand, peeling off the skin and exposing the raw nerves. Danby for the Bangor, *Maine Daily News* depicted the wall, the memorial where I stood with General Smith in 2000, and a voice (let us call it the voice from the wall) because in the cartoon there is no one (no one alive, anyway) standing anywhere around. And the voice from the wall sighs, "In retrospect, I wish McNamara had spoken up earlier." When policymakers make mistakes, they should speak up then, not after the blood and treasure has been spilled.

The Vietnam Memorial is featured in another cartoon in 1995. This time it's the artwork of Deering for the *Arkansas Democrat Gazette.* Two aging veterans are standing at the wall, one leans on a cane, the other is stenciling the name of a fallen comrade off the wall. The cane-holding veteran remarks, "Robert McNamara issued a statement saying our involvement in Vietnam was wrong." And there's the ghostly voice from the wall, again, uttering, "Now he tells us."

A third cartoon is by the *Charlotte Observer's* Kevin Siers. The scene is a well-known one from America's longest war, a Vietnamese civilian fleeing her burning village, *circa* 1968, an eleven-year-old girl burned with napalm, horror and pain on her face. Tears engulfing others fleeing, as an observing Robert McNamara, book in hand, comments, "Oops."

There is something almost surreal about how we Americans sort through the ashes of our Vietnam experience. As we have seen, we do not accept losing gracefully. In a way, this is one of our national talents. We do not like to lose-in sports, in politics, in business, in love, in war. I kept that national trait in mind as I prepared *The First Mistake.* And it is almost like we were shocked to hear Robert McNamara, one of the old coaches of America's team, admit the obvious, in retrospect. The troubling story documented in the 148 boxes of *The Pentagon Papers* further unnerves us. We are aghast, "Our government lied to us from the beginning." Stunned by the truth.

McNamara tried to explain the mistakes in his book. He writes, "People are human, they are fallible. I concede with painful candor and a heavy heart that the adage applies to me and to my generation of American leadership regarding Vietnam." Earlier in the book, the former policymaker admits, "we were terribly wrong. (This is) the book I planned never to write (but) we owe it to future generations to explain why (we were wrong)." I contend from our vantage point in the Twenty-first Century, "we were terribly wrong from the start." Contrition is good for the soul, and McNamara shed, in front of Diane Sawyer during a "Prime Time Live" interview, a few tears over his role in this terrible conflict.

But there was less than 100% contrition by McNamara as he promoted *In Retrospect*. He identifies four other people or groups who deserve blame for plunging America into the rice paddies of Southeast Asia. He identifies Dwight Eisenhower and comments, "He left the White House with a certain inner satisfaction from laying a potentially intractable problem in Kennedy's lap." But cannot commanders-in-chief re-assess?

McNamara observes that it was Sen. Joseph McCarthy's fault. The Wisconsin senator forced numerous state department experts to run for cover in the 1950s during the Red Scare. With these Asian specialists gone, the former defense secretary explains, "(Kennedy and Johnson policymakers) found ourselves setting policy for a region that was terra incognito." I suggest that that was true a decade earlier; the world beyond our borders often bewilders us, and that has nothing to do with Joe McCarthy. Are there not rationale policymakers willing to offer wise advice?

Then, McNamara identifies Arizona Senator Barry Goldwater as one of those who plunges us into the Vietnam quagmire. In one of McNamara's passages, he praises LBJ as "a model of moderation and restraint." But, throughout the 1964 presidential campaign the GOPs Goldwater "took a hard line on Vietnam...." Apparently, Johnson's "moderation and re-straint" prevented a nuclear Holocaust in Southeast Asia. As I stress in

The First Mistake, Johnson was determined to do what the Kennedy boys could not do in Vietnam, and McNamara was along for most of the ride. It is incredulous to blame a presidential candidate who lost in a landslide.

Finally, McNamara blames the joint chiefs of staff because the generals were always pushing to bomb Hanoi back into the stone age. But, one of the attributes of a republic is that civilians oversee the military from the White House and Capitol Hill. One of our grievances in 1776 was the standing army of the Mother Country quartered among us. As we have seen, the line of those to blame for the Vietnam War is a long one, including many people who should have known better, and it stretches back to the 1940s when the first error was made.

FINDING OUR WAY

"We should get out, but I don't know any way to get out."
—Senator Richard Russell to President Lyndon Johnson, 1963

THIS STUDY OF America's Vietnam experience focuses on the chaotic period stretching from the end of World War II, with a dying Franklin Roosevelt, an untested and inexperienced vice president, Vichy troops mingled among defeated Japanese soldiers throughout Indochina, a towering figure of Charles De Gaulle dreaming of France's redemption, Office of Strategic Services operatives cultivating Ho Chi Minh and Vo Giap, the re-establishment of a French Asian empire, the deepening abyss which climaxed at Dien Bien Phu ,and concludes with the United States stepping forward, or perhaps swaggering forward to take France's place in the first decade of the Cold War.

The thesis of *The First Mistake* is that, in 1944-1945, we missed an opportunity to participate in the rise of a nationalist system in Vietnam, although it had communist blood in its veins. We erred in not being able to separate Ho and Giap from Stalin and Mao. The frigid winds of the Cold War, blowing in those confusing days of 1945, engulfed Harry Truman and his policymakers' containment efforts and mutated into the tsunami of the flawed Domino Theory. If we failed to support the French, the high tides of communism would stain all of Asia red and then make their way in a tidal wave across the Pacific Ocean. We seemed to have amnesia about our own revolutionary history and our colonial war for self-determination. We considered ourselves and our experience exceptional. So, we spent our blood and treasure propping up the NEW French Asian empire because, we reasoned, at least they were not stooges of the Kremlin. It mattered little that we allowed the "milking" to resume.

For nearly a decade, 1945-1954, we were enablers, burning the bridges which, the OSS agents had built to the Viet Minh and casting our lot with the French, who returned to their oppressive management of the people and economy of Vietnam, "milking" them yet again. And then, as the previous chapters tell us, it became OUR turn, with the establishment of Strategic Hamlets, search and destroy missions, inaccurate body counts, the escalation of boots-American boots-on the ground, and presidents who found themselves unable to explain the strategic value of Vietnam to our citizens or correct the mistake of 1945. The milk became tainted with American blood. This horrible story unfolds page after page in the pilfered pages of *The Pentagon Papers* and the delayed memoirs of Robert McNamara.

While John F. Kennedy's presidency was tragically cut short by the gunfire in Dallas, it is debatable what his plans were for American involvement in Vietnam if he had lived to be re-elected in 1964. In the last month of his life, he allowed Vietnamese generals to topple Diem and murder him and his brother, the husband of the acerbic Madame Nhu. His successor, Lyndon Johnson, certainly tumbled down the slippery slope in Southeast Asia. The Texan was determined, as he said, "To not be the first American president to lose a war." In a symbolic sense, Johnson's name could be added to the memorial in Washington. He had seen war in the Pacific Theater during the Second World War as he flew along on a navy mission which encountered Japanese planes, earning for Congressman Johnson a silver star commendation. He enjoyed embellishing the military service of his ancestors in the 1846-1848 Mexican War. Assuming the presidency after the tragedy of Dallas, LBJ was determined to leave his own brand on the White House. His disdain for "the Harvards" and his boast "to do what the Kennedy boys could never do" in Vietnam derailed his plans for a Great Society and ripped this country apart. Hubris, ignorance, arrogance, tragedy, lack of account-ability, the swagger of American exceptionalism.

Jacqueline Kennedy and her stunned young children had barely vacated the Executive Mansion in late 1963 before Johnson's attention turned to Vietnam. In a December 1963 telephone conversation with Georgia Senator Richard B. Russell, the discussion turned to Indochina. Johnson had always cultivated older mentors like Franklin Roosevelt ("He was like a daddy to me"), Speaker of the United States House of Representatives "Mr. Sam" Rayburn, and the courtly wizard of Winder, Georgia. Russell, the cagey leg-islator, reminded the new commander-in-chief, "I tried my best to keep them (Truman, Eisenhower, and Kennedy) from going into Laos and Vietnam… said we'd never get out-be in there fifty years from now." Assessing the com-plex predicament which his mentee had inherited, Russell confided, "We should get out, but I don't know any way to get out." And the situation dete-riorated. By May 1964, the two men were conversing again with the senator lamenting, "It's the damn worst mess I ever saw.…We're just in the quick-sand-up to our necks." This book attempts to explain how we became stuck.

The First Mistake is written for the men and women who stood with me and General Homer Smith at the Vietnam Memorial during the 2000 cer-emony. "The worst mess" was not their creation, and as I remarked on that spring morning, the mistakes were not theirs. As *Vietnam Magazine* said in a April 2000 review about *White Christmas In April: The Collapse Of South Vietnam, 1975* , "This book is a fitting tribute to all those Americans who did what was right, even when their government told them it was wrong." But the spark which fueled *The First Mistake* was my determination to explore the missed opportunity of 1945 and how misguided American poli-cymakers allowed the return of French colonialism to deepen our nation's involvement in the region as the Cold War intensified. Ho and Giap, who had assisted *The Deer Team,* felt betrayed, "milked" yet again.

This book, also, should be of use to college and university students born long after the siege at Dien Bien Phu, the Gulf of Tonkin Incident, the battle of Ia Drang, the Tet Offensive, and the evacuation of Saigon. Those students, many born in the Twenty-First Century, need to be reminded that, as exceptional as the United States is, miscalculations can be catastrophic. Indeed, Ho Chi Minh was a communist, but his nationalistic tendencies fermented for decades. And French colonialism, as Roosevelt said, had robbed Vietnam of control of its own destiny. The compilers of *The Pentagon Papers* raised the issue: "Is Ho Chi Minh An Asian Tito?" As difficult as it is to admit, not EVERYONE wants to be like us. Nevertheless, there are events in our country's own past, such as the American Revolution, which should help us grasp that EVERYONE wants to be independent. That was true in 1776, and it was true in 1945. It became our costly first mistake in the Vietnam War.

"The Vietnam Veterans Memorial in Washington, D.C."

"During nearly a century of French colonial rule, the architecture, political system, society, and economy of Vietnam was transformed by France. In Ben Tre, these government buildings have now become a museum."

*"The natural beauty of the Mekong Delta and what was called
Cochinchina during the colonial era is timeless."*

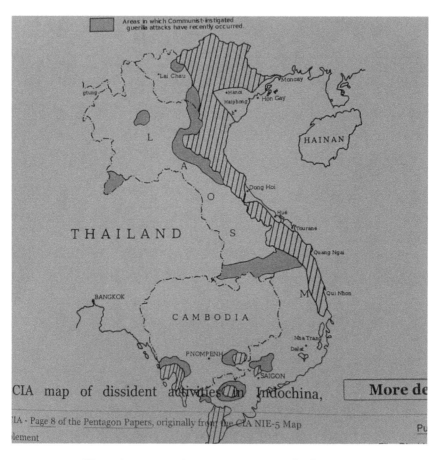

Areas in which Communist-instigated
guerilla attacks have recently occurred.

CIA map of dissident activities in Indochina,

CIA - Page 8 of the Pentagon Papers, originally from the CIA NIE-5 Map

More de

"From the Pentagon Papers , a top secret study of America's presence in Vietnam, this map is from 1950. "

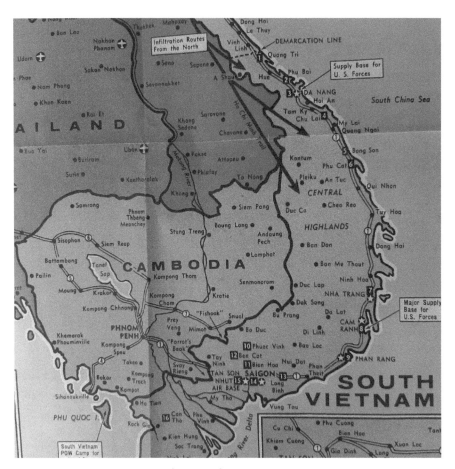

"Color map of Vietnam , 1970."

"White Lotus Plants , Vietnam's official flower. "

"By 1965, the United States was fully committed to defeating the communists in South Vietnam."

"After France was defeated in 1954 at Dien Bien Phu, the Viet Minh(Viet
Cong), the communist guerrilla military, was fought by American forces."

"When South Vietnam's President Ngo Dinh Diem, a Roman Catholic, and his brother and powerful sister-in-law, Madame Nhu, battled communists and Buddhists, unrest erupted in the streets of Saigon. Here, a monk commits suicide in 1963."

"The influencial Madame Nhu, sister-in-law to President Diem."

"American operatives formed a close relationship with Ho Chi Minh and Vo Nguyen Giap during World War II as they rescued American pilots and prisoners of war held by the Japanese. Here, the Deer Team of the Office of Strategic Services sits with Ho and Giap, 1945. Ho told the Americans he was a nationalist as well as a communist."

*"In the last year of his life, American President Franklin D. Roosevelt
spoke against the re-instatement of French colonialism in Vietnam.
He contended that France had 'milked' its Asian colony."*

CHRONOLOGY

S AND IN HISTORY'S hourglass allows us to understand how time guides us through a story. In America's longest war, that sand began flowing during World War II and it flows quickly. I have selected a few of the key dates which demonstrate the process which fueled our increasing involvement in Indochina.

- May 1941-Viet Minh created by Vietnamese communists and non-communists as an organization advocating self-determination and opposition to the Vichy government and Japanese military.

- December 7, 1941- Japanese attack on Pearl Harbor.

- 1944-First OSS contacts with Ho Chi Minh at his base in China.

- August 25, 1944-Paris is liberated from the Nazis.

- November 1944- Franklin Roosevelt wins a fourth term as president.

- February 1945-The Yalta Conference includes Roosevelt, Winston Churchill, and Joseph Stalin.

- March 9, 1945- Japanese overthrow the remnants of the French government in Indochina.

- April 12, 1945- Roosevelt dies in Warm Springs, Georgia and is succeeded by Vice President Harry Truman.

- May 8, 1945-Germany surrenders to the Allies.

- June 1945-OSS operatives strengthen their ties to Ho Chi Minh

- August 1945-Atomic Bombs used on Japanese cities of Hiroshima and Nagasaki. Japan surrenders, August 15.

- August 25, 1945-Emperor Bao Dai abdicates in favor of Ho Chi Minh.

- September 2, 1945-Ho Chi Minh proclaims the independence of Indochina in Hanoi.

- September 1945-Clashes begin between French and Viet Minh.

- March 1946-French troops arrive in Haiphong.

- July 1946-Ho pleads his case for independence in Paris.

- November and December 1946-Clashes continue between Viet Minh and French military.

- 1947- Containment, Truman Doctrine, and Marshall Plan formulated.

- November 1948-Truman elected president.

- September 1949-Soviet Union detonates its atomic bomb.

- 1949-After years of conflict, Mao topples Chiang in China.

- January 1950- Both Communist China and Soviet Union recognize Ho Chi Minh's regime in Vietnam.

- June 25, 1950-North Korea invades South Korea, beginning three years of hostilities, a "police action" by the United Nations.

- June 1950-United States flies military supplies to Saigon.

- January 1951-French military has successes against Viet Minh.

- March 1952-Aid by United States increases.

- November 1952-After promising to go to Korea, Dwight Eisenhower elected president.

- May 1953-French General Henri Navarre appointed commander.

- July 1953-Armistice signed between communist North Korea and non-communist South Korea.

- September 1953-American assistance to French efforts against Viet Minh increases.

- November 1953-French begin setting up base at Dien Bien Phu.

- March 13, 1954-Viet Minh assault on Dien Bien Phu commences.

- April 1954-Dien Bien Phu under siege, U.S. wants congressional approval for bombing.

- May 7, 1954-Dien Bien Phu falls to communists.

- June 16, 1954-Emperor Bao Dai appoints Ngo Dinh Diem prime minister of Vietnam.

- July 21, 1954-In Geneva, cease fire agreed among warring sides in Vietnam. Including a division of Ho's North Vietnam and Diem's South Vietnam with elections promised within two years.

- August 1954-Exodus of Roman Catholics from north to south.

- September 1954-SEATO formed in Philippines.

- February 1955-American advisors begin instructing South Vietnam military.

- August 1955-Diem rejects negotiations with Ho.

- November 1956-Eisenhower re-elected.

- May 1959-Ho Chi Minh Trail begins transporting weapons and personnel into South Vietnam.

- July 1959-Viet Minh kill two Americans at Bien Hoa.

- May 1960-Military assistance to South Vietnam increases.

- November 1960-John F. Kennedy elected president.

- December 1960- Viet Minh renamed Viet Cong, National Liberation Front created.

- May 1961- Vice-President Lyndon Johnson visits Saigon, Kennedy approves special forces operations against North Vietnam.

- November 1961-Kennedy Administration increases aid to South Vietnam.

KEY PEOPLE

- Bao Dai- Last emperor of Vietnam, cooperated with Japanese during World War II, abdicated 1945, returned under French and ruled as chief of state until Ngo Dinh Diem came to power after 1954 Geneva Conference.

- Ho Chi Minh (Nguyen Tat Thanh)- roamed the world as a young man, including stops in the United States and training in Moscow, attempted to meet with President Woodrow Wilson at 1919 Paris Peace Conference, founded the Indochinese Communist Party in Hong Kong and returned to Vietnam in 1941, worked with operatives from the Office of Strategic Services during World War II, proclaimed Vietnam's independence from France in 1945 and fought the French for next nine years.

- Ngo Dinh Diem-Roman Catholic anti-communist, rejected the elections which had been mandated at the 1954 Geneva Conference, became prime minister of South Vietnam in 1955 and allowed his unpopular brother (Ngo Dinh Nhu) and sister-in-law to create tensions with the Buddhists, assassinated with American complicity in 1963.

- Pham Van Dong-one of the founders of the Indochinese Communist Party, close to Ho Chi Minh, served as Ho's prime minister, and represented the communists at the 1954 Geneva Conference.

- Vo Nguyen Giap-superb tactician, created the Viet Minh military which ultimately defeated the French at Dien Bien Phu, worked with the OSS agents during World War II.

- Henri Navarre- French commander in Vietnam as the final battle approached in 1953-1954 at Dien Bien Phu, a site he selected.

- Henri Philippe Petain-World War I French hero, installed by Axis Powers over Vichy France, including France's Indochinese colony.

- Dean Acheson-U. S. Secretary of State 1949-1952 urged President Truman to supply aid to French.

- A. Peter Dewey-OSS agent, killed by Viet Minh in 1945, becoming first American to die in Vietnam.

- John Foster Dulles- U.S. Secretary of State 1953-1959, strong anticommunist, promoted assistance to France, failed to persuade Eisenhower to use nuclear weapons to breakthe siege of Dien Bien Phu.

- George F. Kennan-as State Department official in 1947 became architect of communist containment.

- James F. Byrnes-Truman's first Secretary of State favored hard-nosed resistance to the Soviet Union around the globe.

- George C. Marshall- as Truman's Secretary of State in 1947-1948 and later Defense Secretary, favored economic aid to bolster non-communist elements, namesake of the Marshall Plan.

- Mao Zedong-driving Chiang off the mainland of China in 1949, he and his communist ally Joseph Stalin supported Viet Minh.

- Joseph Stalin-Soviet leader until his death in 1953, supported expansion of communism worldwide, including Vietnam.

American Presidents

Franklin D. Roosevelt (1933-1945)

Harry Truman (1945-1953)

Dwight D. Eisenhower (1953-1961)

John F. Kennedy (1961-1963)

Lyndon B. Johnson (1963-1969)

Richard M. Nixon (1969-1974)

Gerald R. Ford (1974-1977)

A NOTE ON SOURCES

THE HISTORIOGRAPHY OF the Vietnam War is voluminous. It begins, as I noted earlier, with *The Pentagon Papers*, thousands of pages of government documents which the Johnson Administration prepared from 1967-1969 describing America's involvement in Indochina from 1940 until the sharp escalation of the mid-1960s. This collection was presented to Secretary of Defense Clark Clifford five days before President Richard Nixon's inauguration. When Daniel Ellsberg made them available to the *New York Times*, a firestorm erupted. Finally, the United States Supreme Court sided with freedom of the press. By then, other newspapers, such as *The Washington Post*, had gained access to the enormous cache of documents which indicted our nation's political establishment, including presidents. Sen. Mike Gravell made available to the public his edition of *The Pentagon Papers*, too. While preparing *The First Mistake*, I found this government study invaluable, especially since the entire collection is now available on-line for researchers.

Materials which Dr. Haynsworth and I used in preparing *White Christmas In April* and *Nixon, Ford And The Abandonment of South Vietnam* were helpful. During our research, we traveled extensively and, as we met with people, it seemed they all wished to share not just memories and impressions but also documents. I kept them all, dusted them off, and assessed what they told us about the war's early years and what went wrong. The Saigon

Mission Association's members were invaluable; many of the members had served multiple tours in Vietnam, and I enjoyed our conversations.

Newspapers are excellent primary sources. I reviewed *The Washington Post, The Washington Star, The New York Times, Le Monde, Paris Match,* and the *Wall Street Journal* from the 1940s to the 1960s. They distinguished themselves in preparing the first draft of history.

In the acknowledgements, I mention several helpful Vietnamese. Additionally, I had the opportunity to interview shortly before his death, my late colleague Haney Howell, who had served as a journalist in Southeast Asia. His observations about how the war looked on CBS News was beneficial.

The papers of American presidents, while some are restricted and some are incomplete, were helpful. The National Archives and the presidential libraries of the key presidents, as well as the Library of Congress have made a considerable number of these documents readily available, on-line. Hearing the voices of Dwight Eisenhower, John Kennedy, Lyndon Johnson, and Richard Nixon on tape is useful. All of these chief executives tried to make since of what our country inherited in Indochina. Harry Truman wrote about that topic in his memoirs, as did Eisenhower, Johnson and Nixon.

To understand Ho Chi Minh, I listened carefully to my Vietnamese contacts. I read media coverage of Ho and General Giap.I studied Vo Nguyen Giap's *Big Victory, Great Task* (New York: Praeger, 1968). I gained a sharp understanding of how nationalism and communism can co-exist. I supplemented that material William Duiker's *Ho Chi Minh* (New York: Hyperion, 2010). I employed a similar approach to appreciating General Charles De Gaulle's wish in 1945 to redeem France. French friends helped as did a reading of Julian Jackson's *De Gaulle* (New York: Belknap, 2018).

The French debacle at Dien Bien Phu is made abundantly clear in Bernard Fall's *Hell In A Very Small Place* (New York: Praeger, 1966) and Ted

Morgan's *Valley Of Death* (New York: Random House, 2010). The French newspapers mentioned above covered the siege well.

Journalist Stanley Karnow's *Vietnam: A History* (New York: Viking, 1983) remains a valuable source. I found its analysis of colonial Indochina especially useful, as was its comprehensive bibliography. Other helpful books were Norm Friedman's *The Fifty Year War* (Annapolis: Naval Institute Press, 2000), Robert Miller and Dennis Wainstock's *Indochina And Vietnam* (New York: Enigma Books, 2013), and Geoffrey Ward and Ken Burns' *The Vietnam War: An Intimate History* (New York: Knopf, 2017).

I found much of enduring value in David Halberstam's *The Best And The Brightest* (New York: Ballantine, 1993), George Herring's *America's Longest War* (New York: McGraw Hill, 1986), Townsend Hoopes' *The Limits Of Intervention* (New York: David McKay, 1970), and Robert McNamara's *In Retrospect* (New York: Little Brown, 1995). Finally, Michael Lind's work *Vietnam War* (New York: Free Press, 1999) continues to intrigue me even though I question its premise.

Photo of Dr. J. Edward Lee, the author

ABOUT THE AUTHOR

A FORMER PRESIDENT OF the South Carolina Historical Association, Dr. J. Edward Lee is professor of history at Winthrop University. He is a thirty-year veteran of the university classroom and has won several awards for innovative teaching, especially in the area of distance learning. He is the author of fifteen other books, including two other ones on the Vietnam War. He has been a media commentator for NBC News, CNN, and NPR. Regularly, he lectures on a wide range of historical topics, ranging from the American presidency to foreign policy to local history. In 2015, he received the State Historic Preservation Award from Governor Nikki Haley for his successful efforts to save the York County Courthouse. From 2002-2020, he was mayor of his hometown of York, S.C.

Lightning Source UK Ltd.
Milton Keynes UK
UKHW021450151220
375215UK00001B/26